MANDALA

Beautiful Mandala Design For Adults

Amazing Design To Relief Your Strees

Here You Get Almost 100 Unique Mandala Design

For Your Relaxation, Making Fun and Show Your Creativity

This Book Belongs To

____

____

____

SAMPLE DESIGN

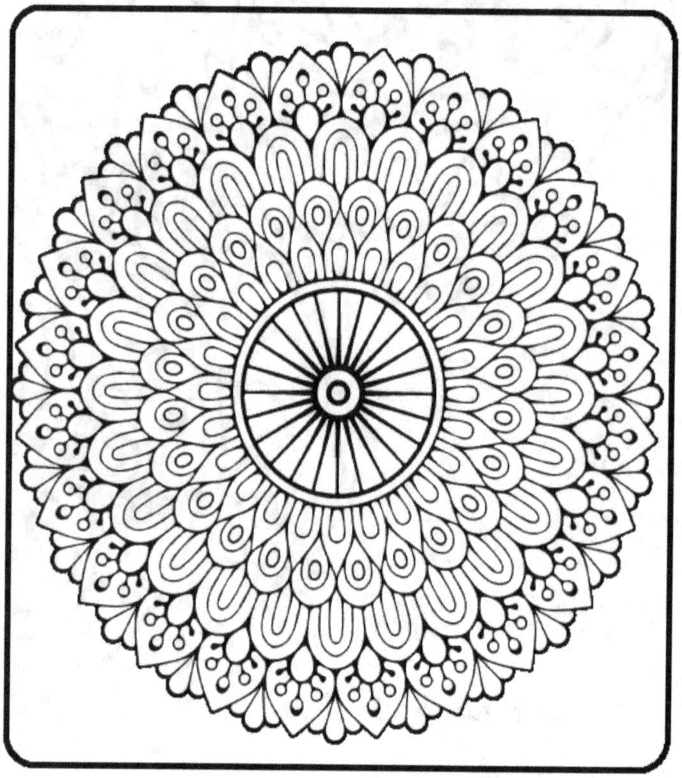

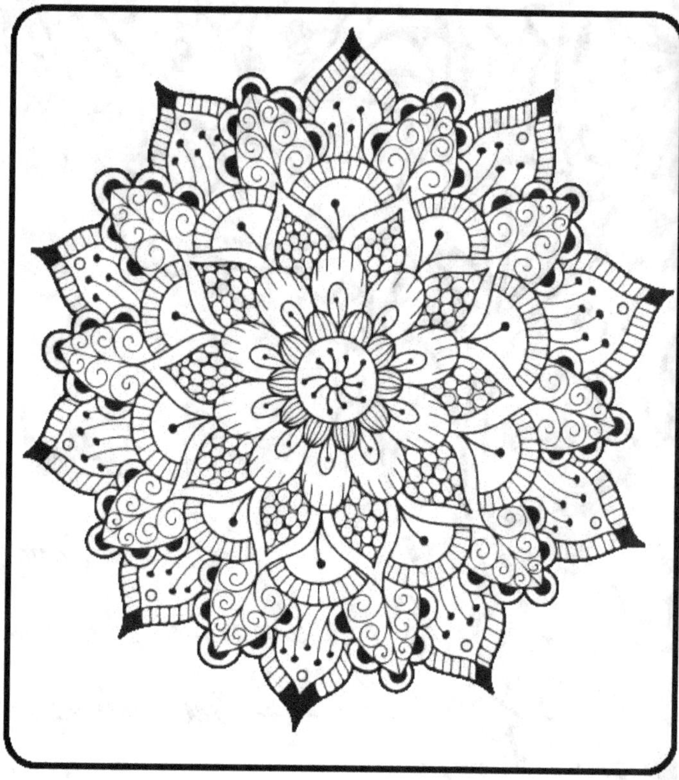

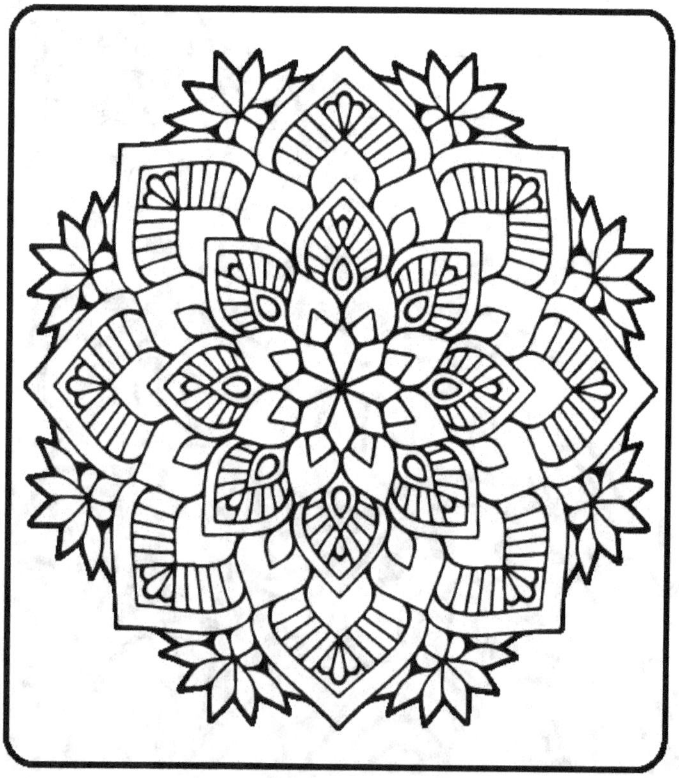

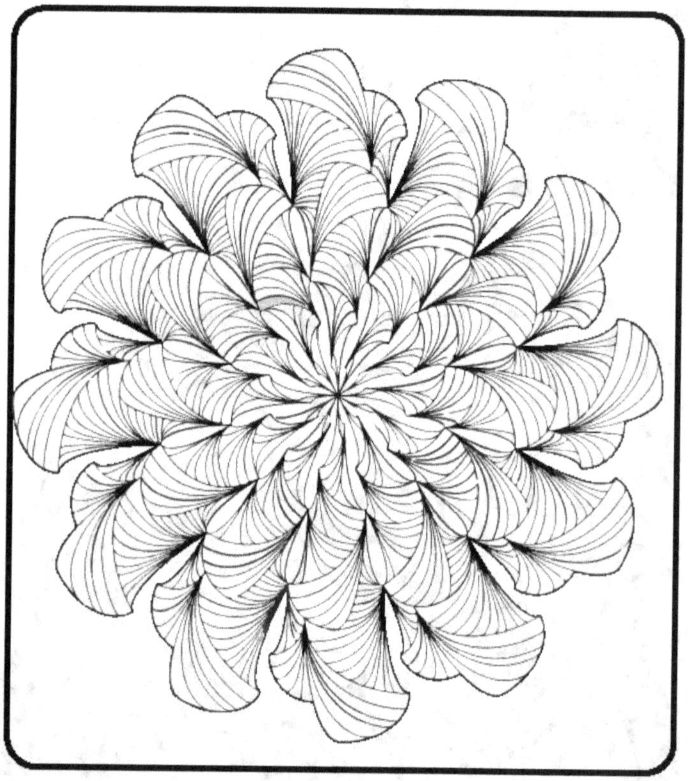

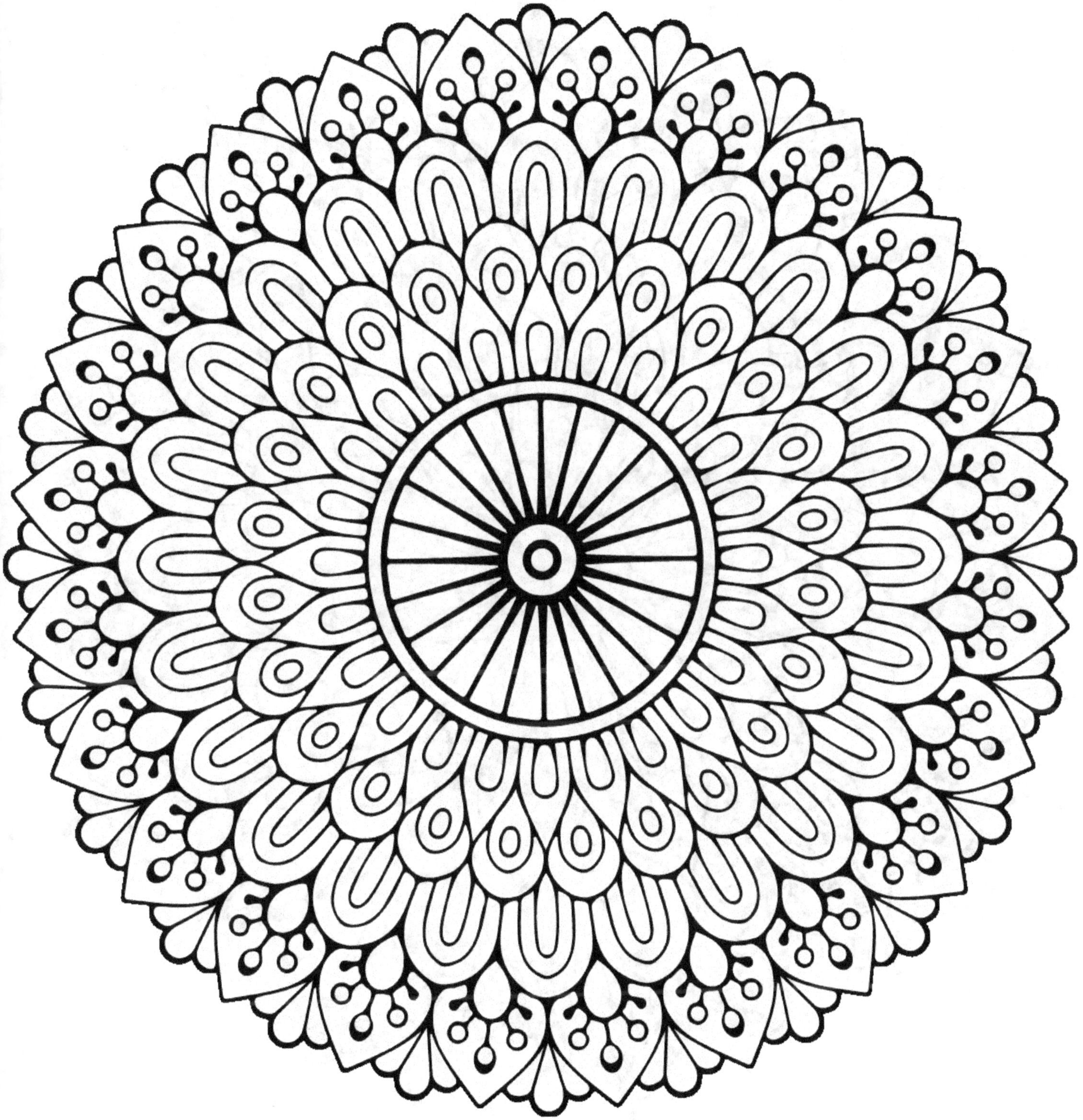

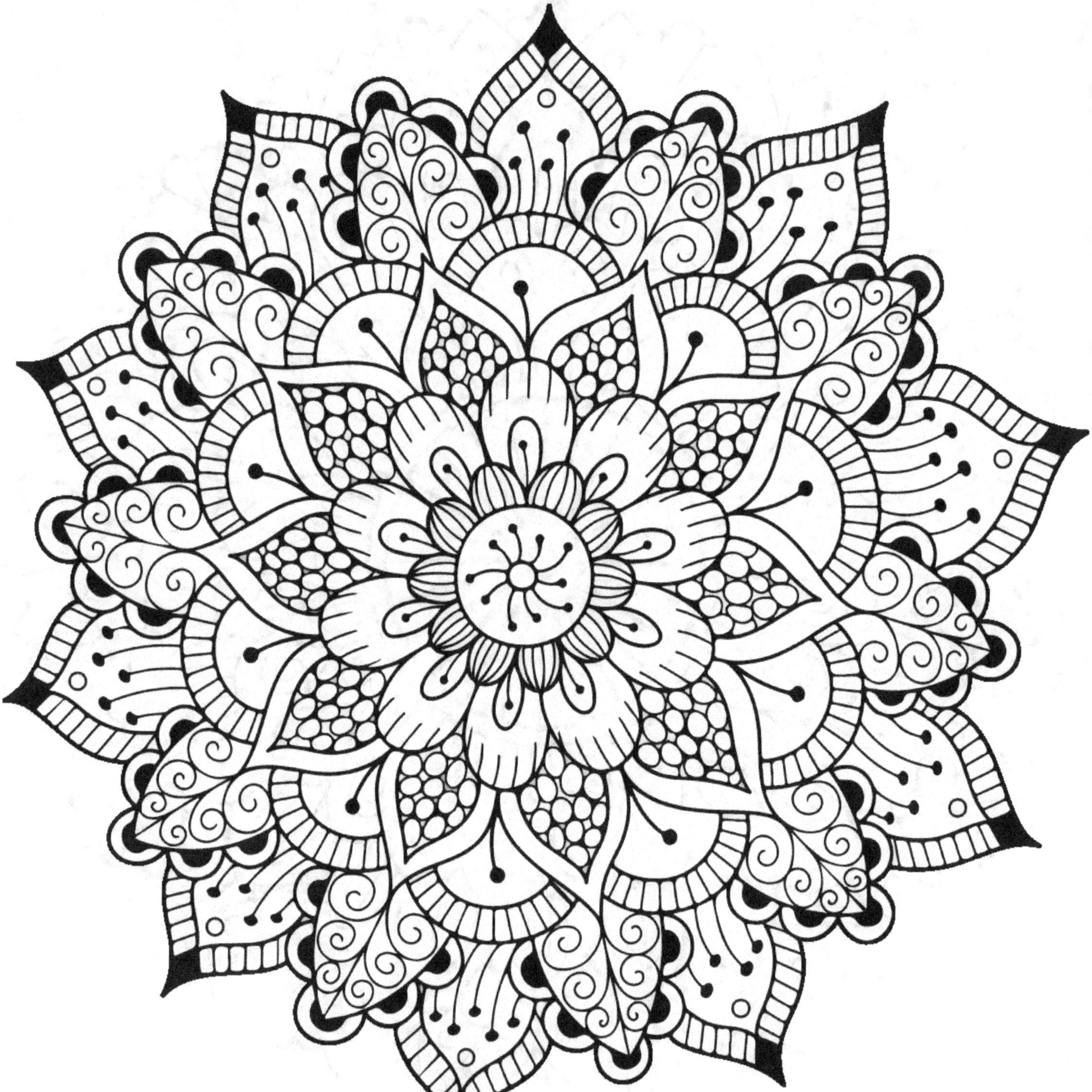

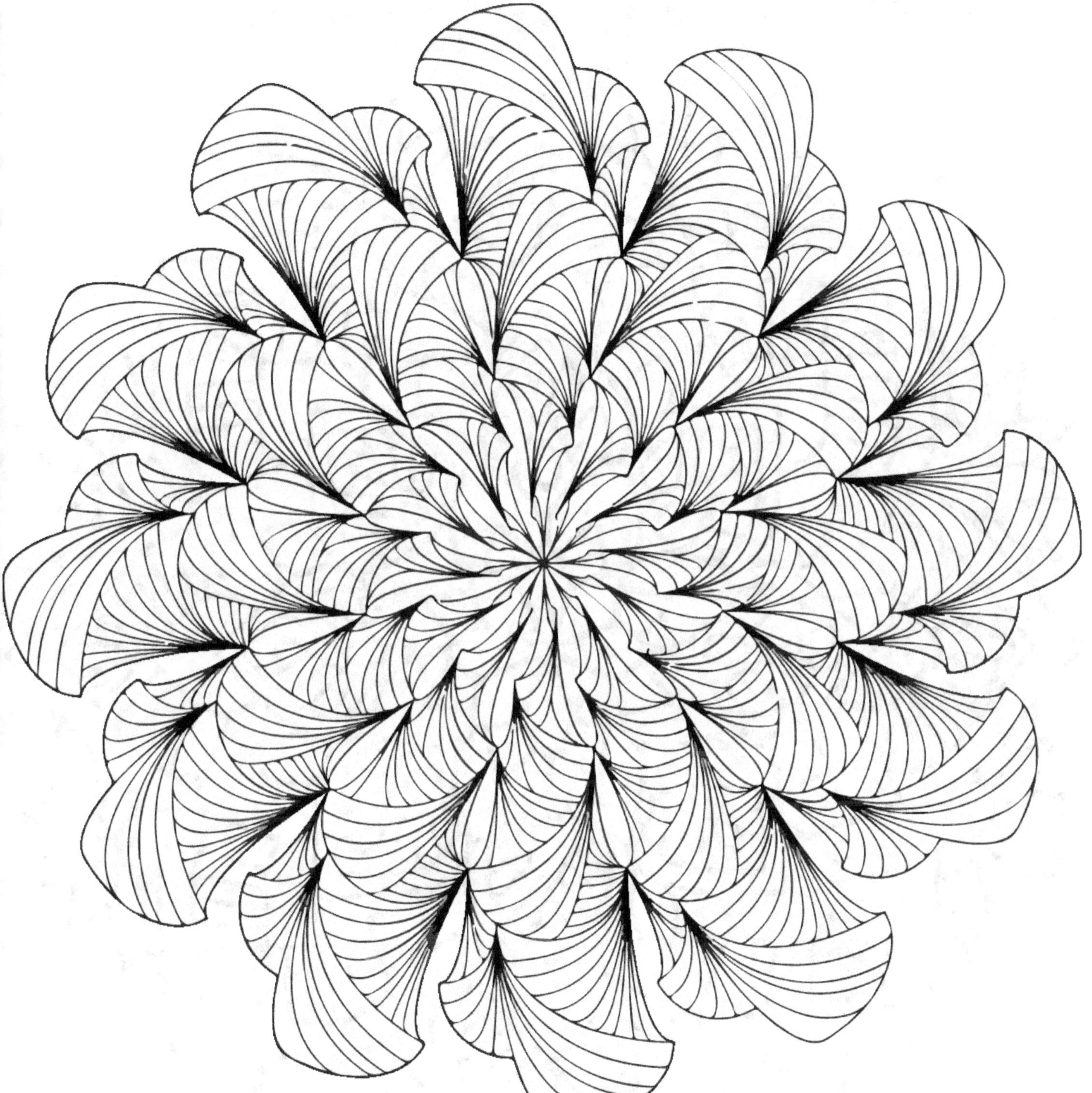

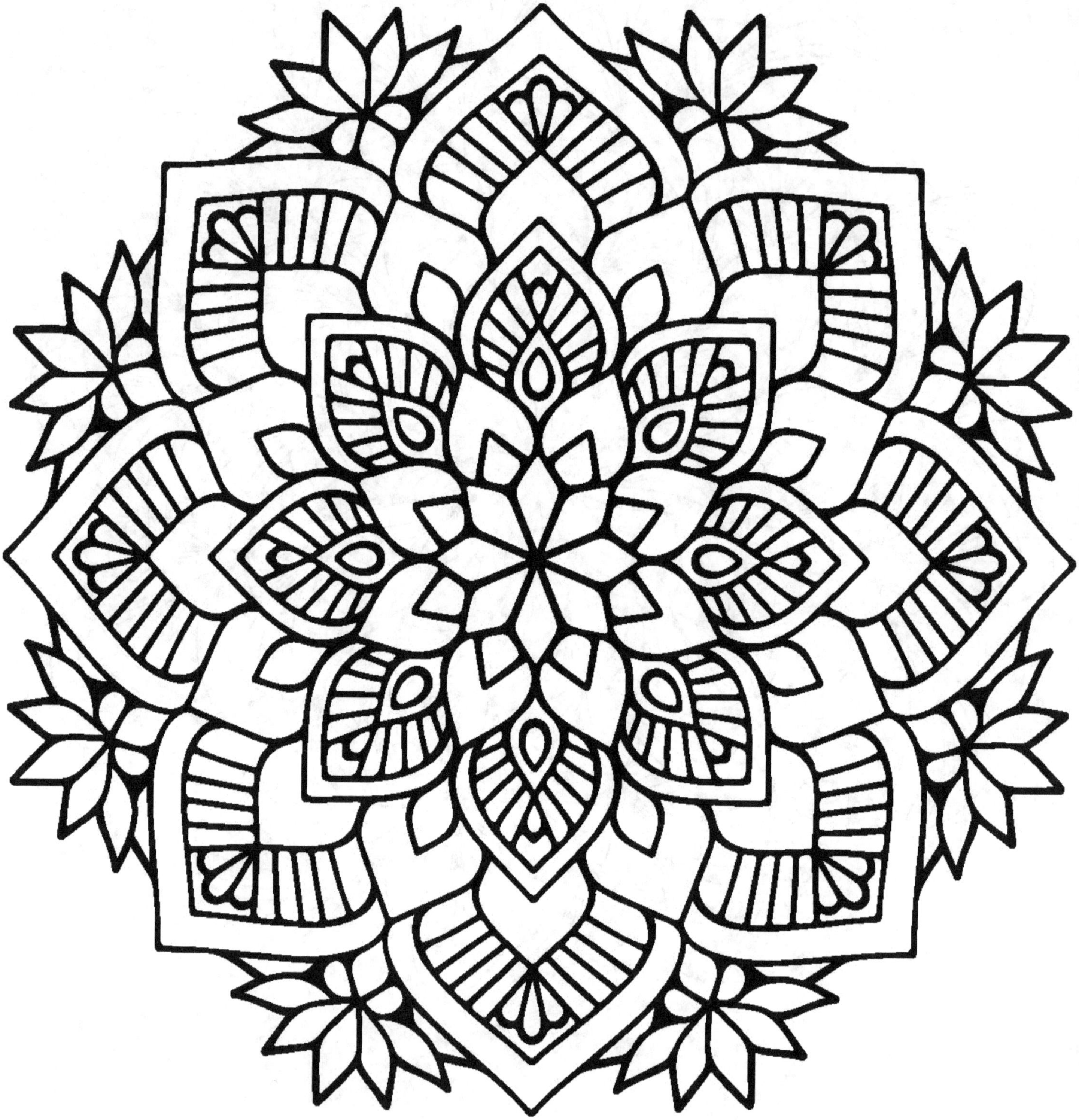

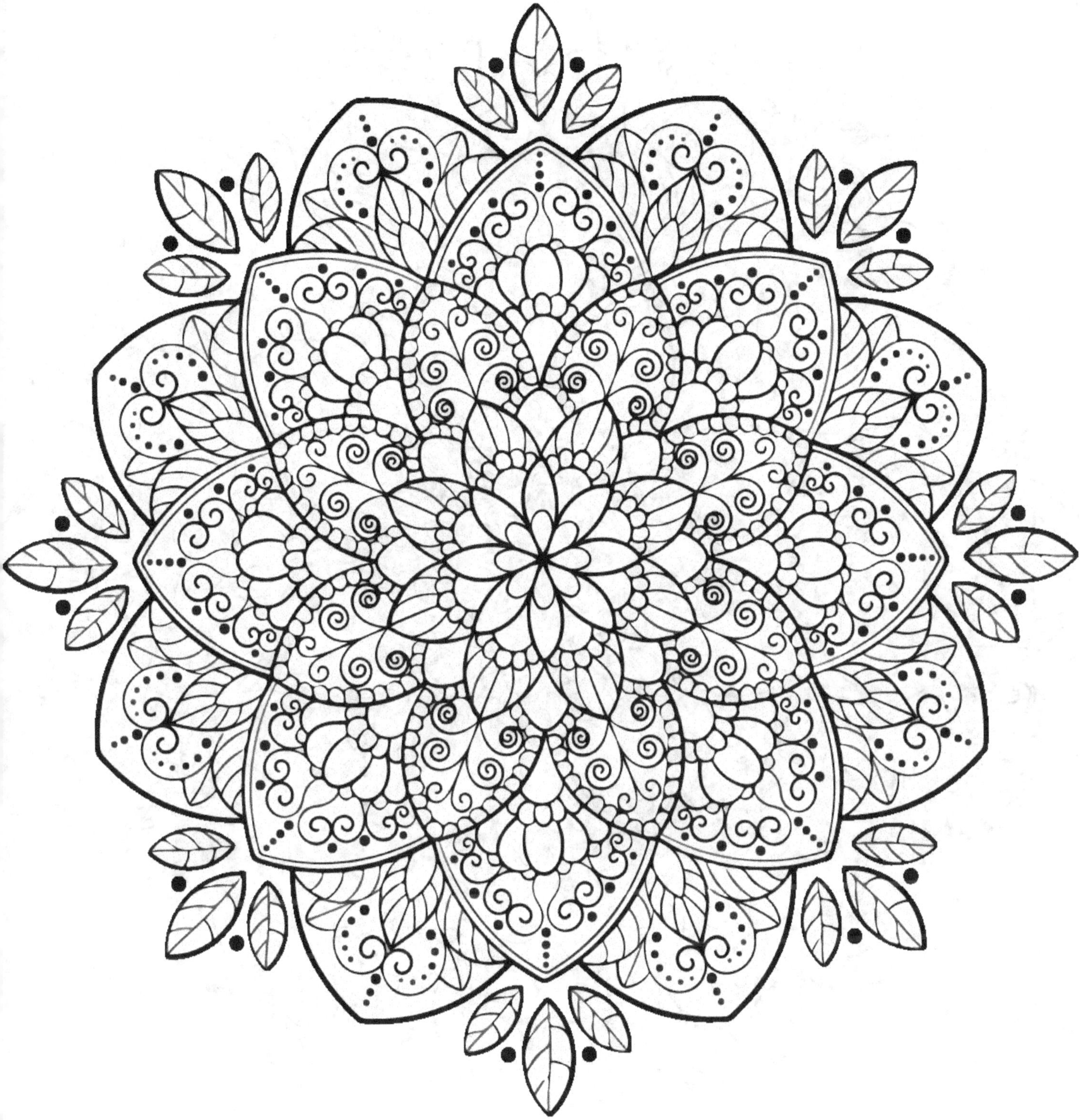

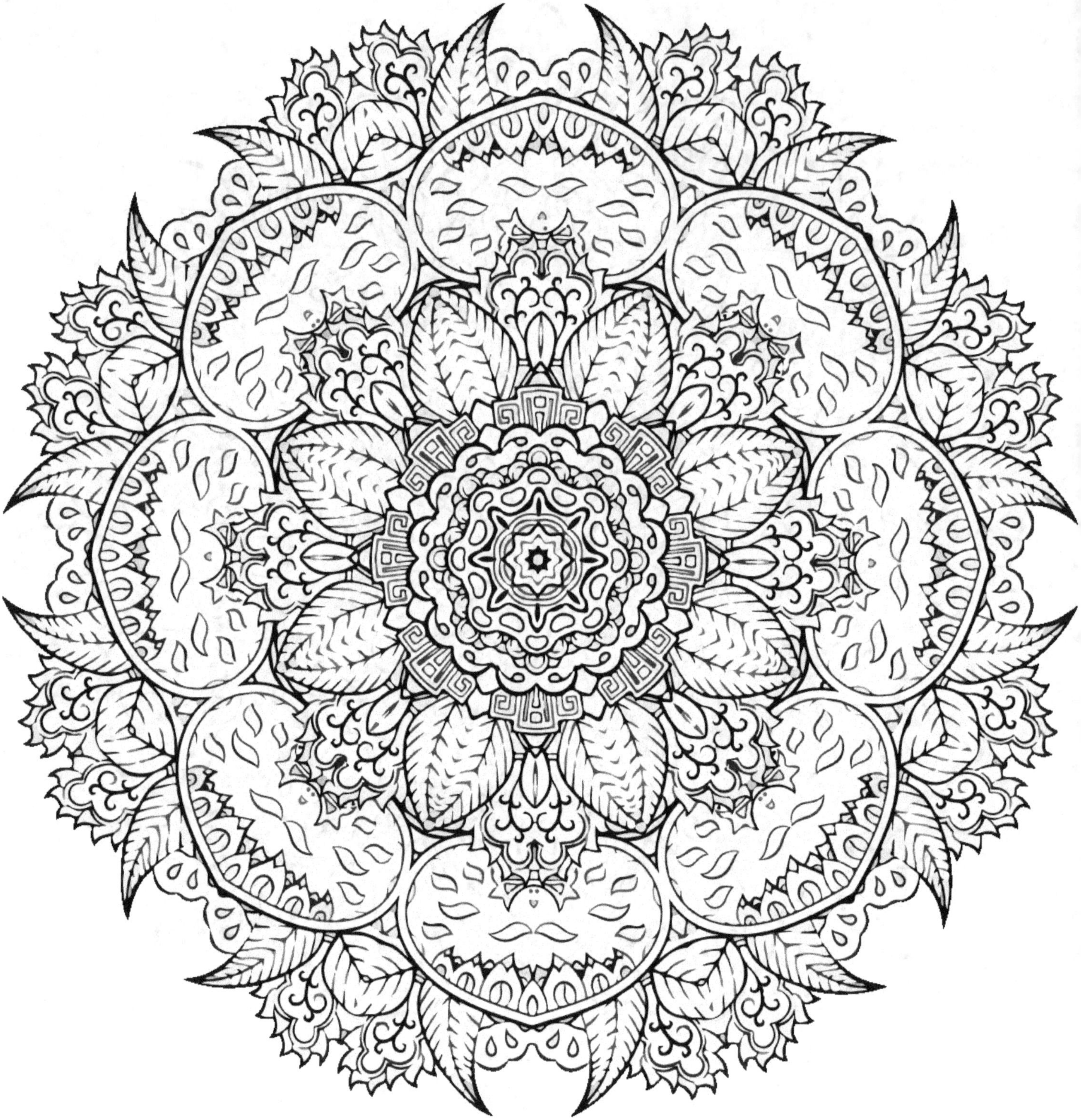

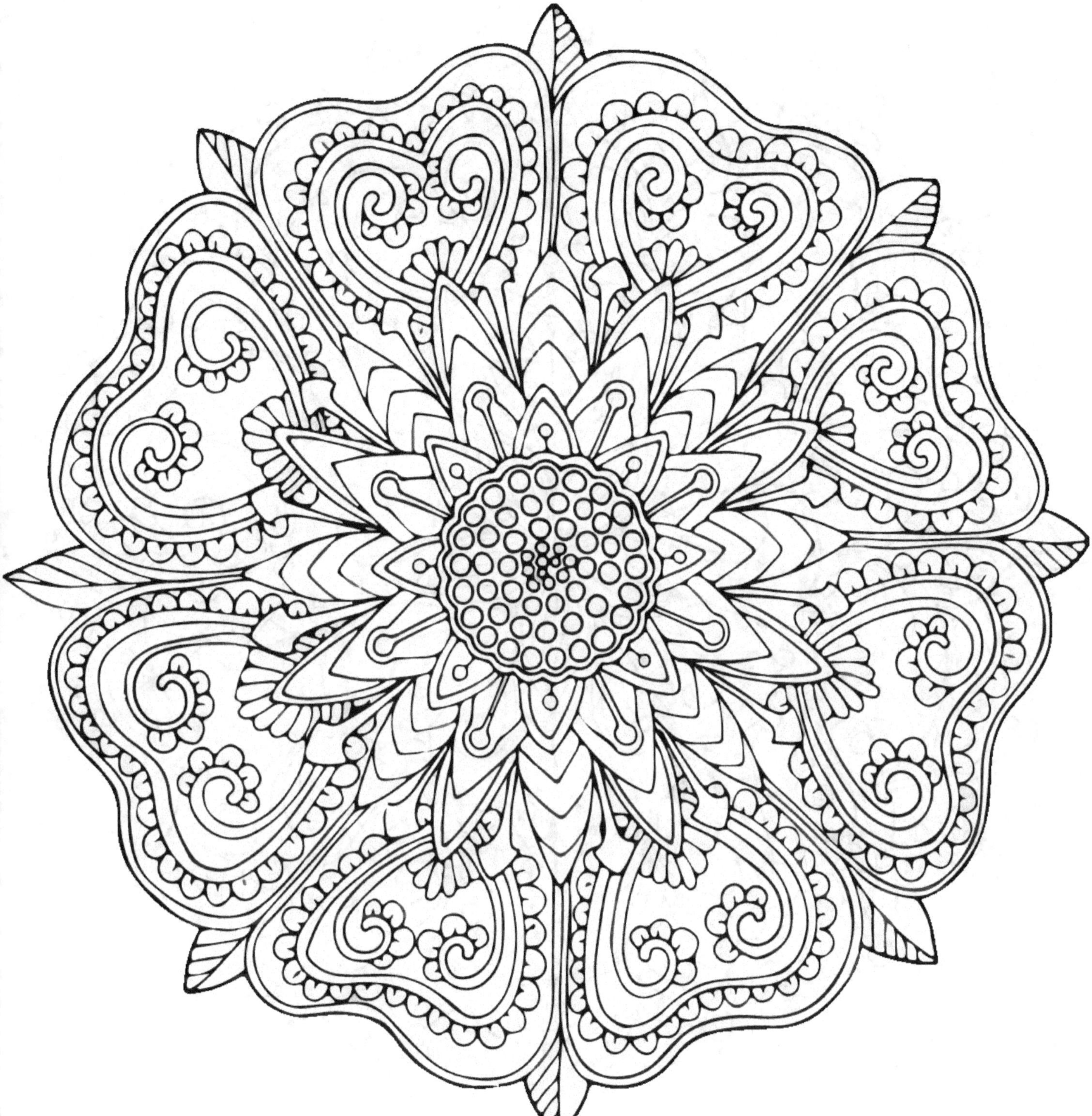

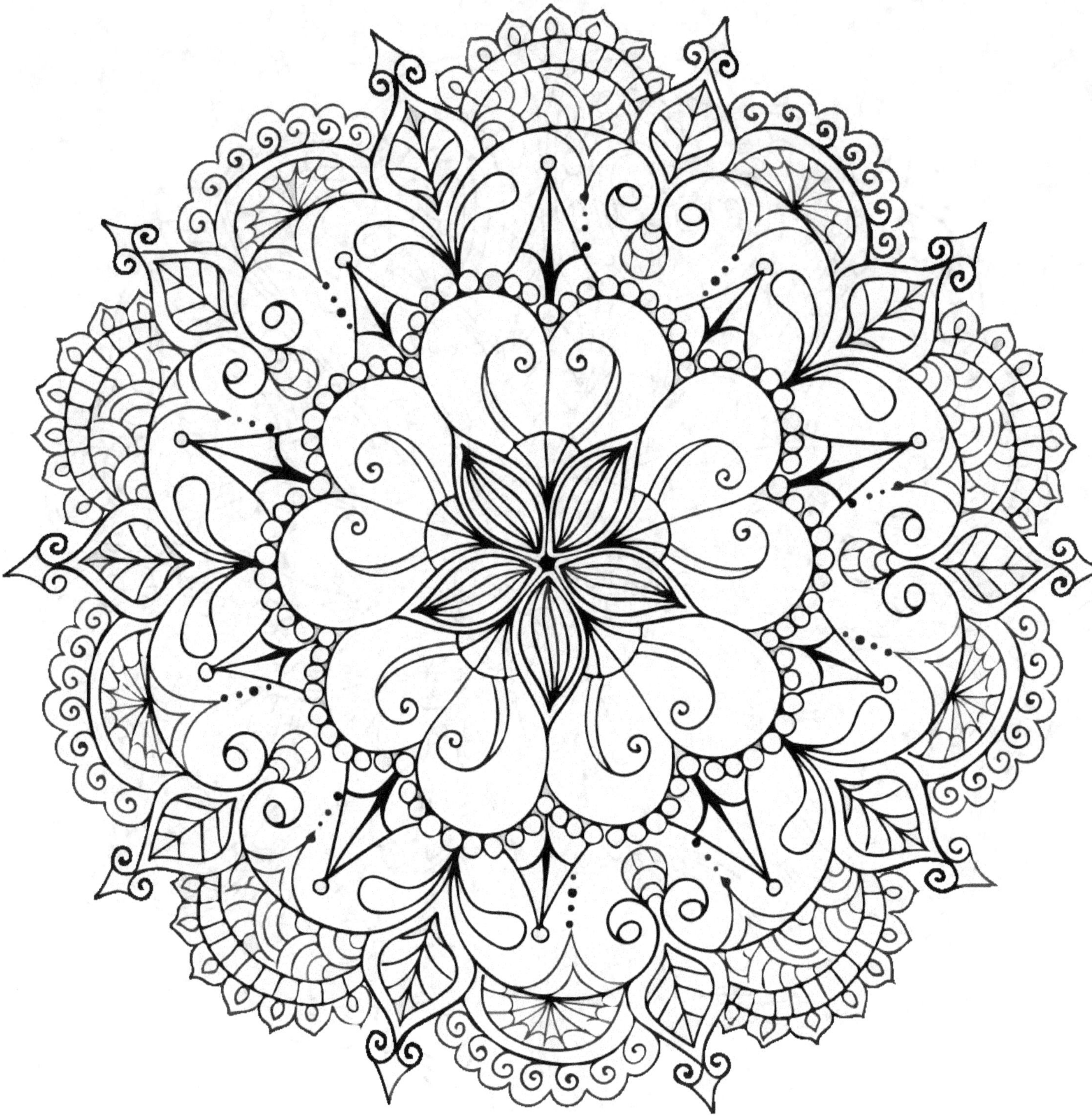

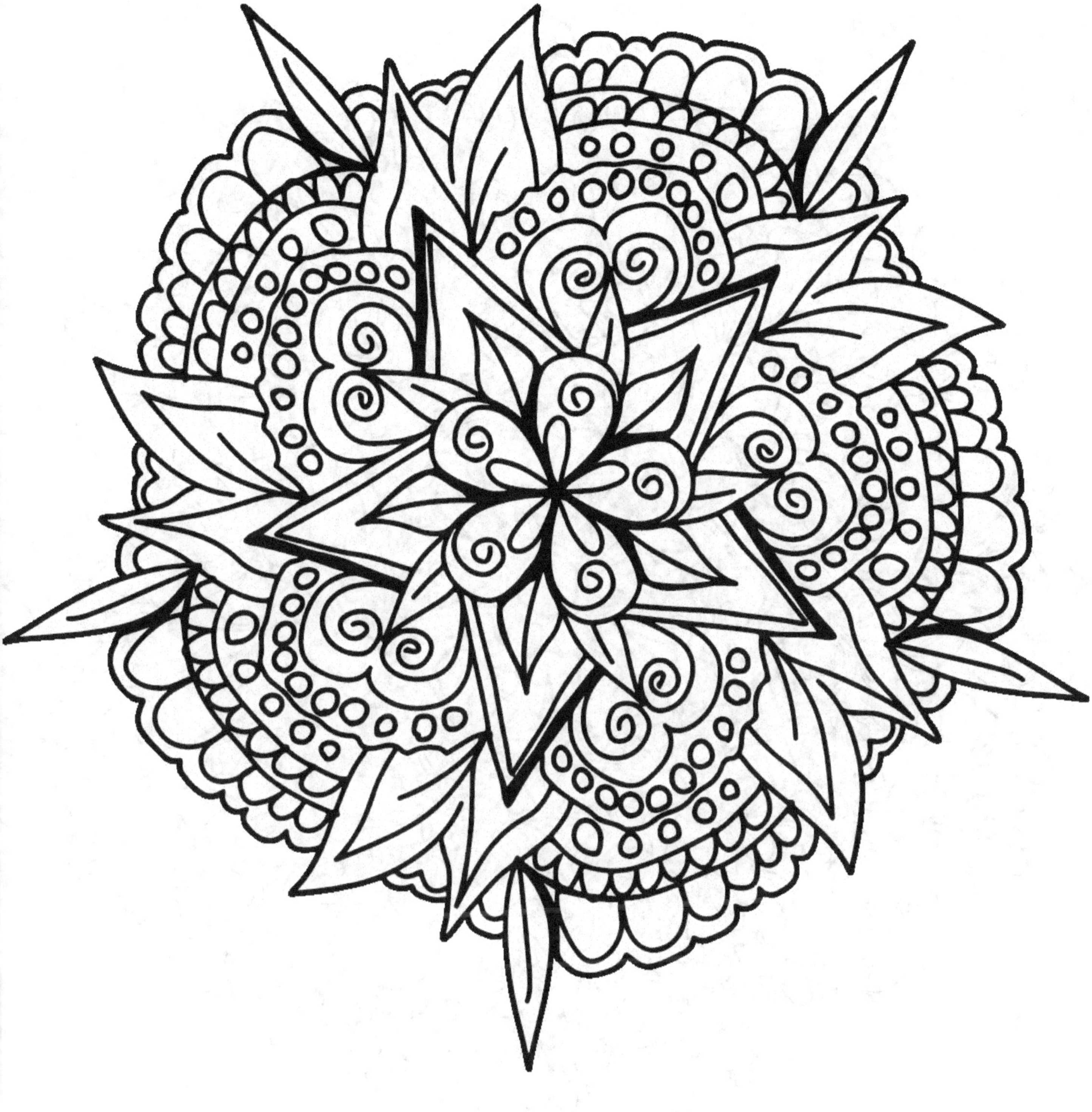

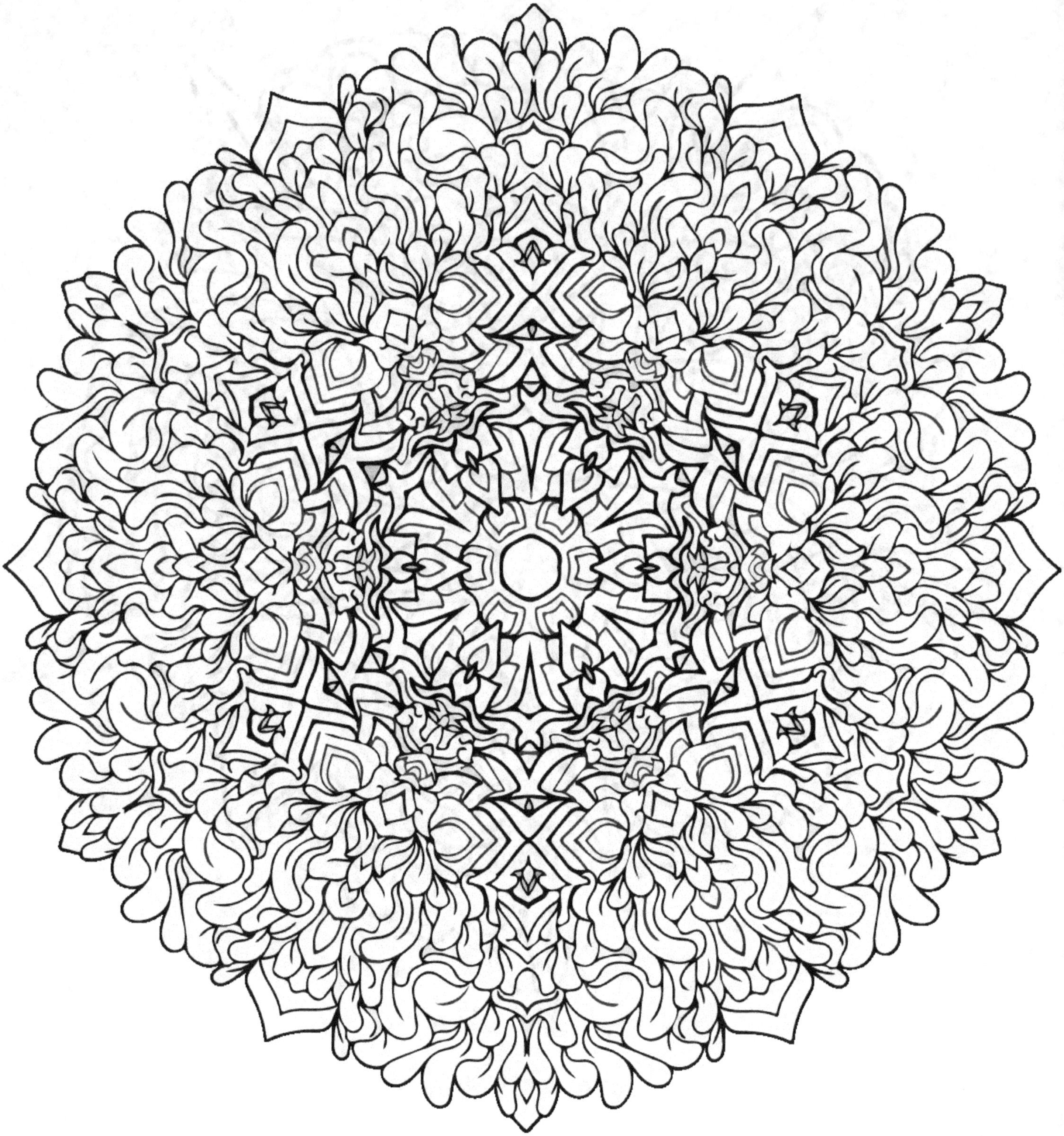

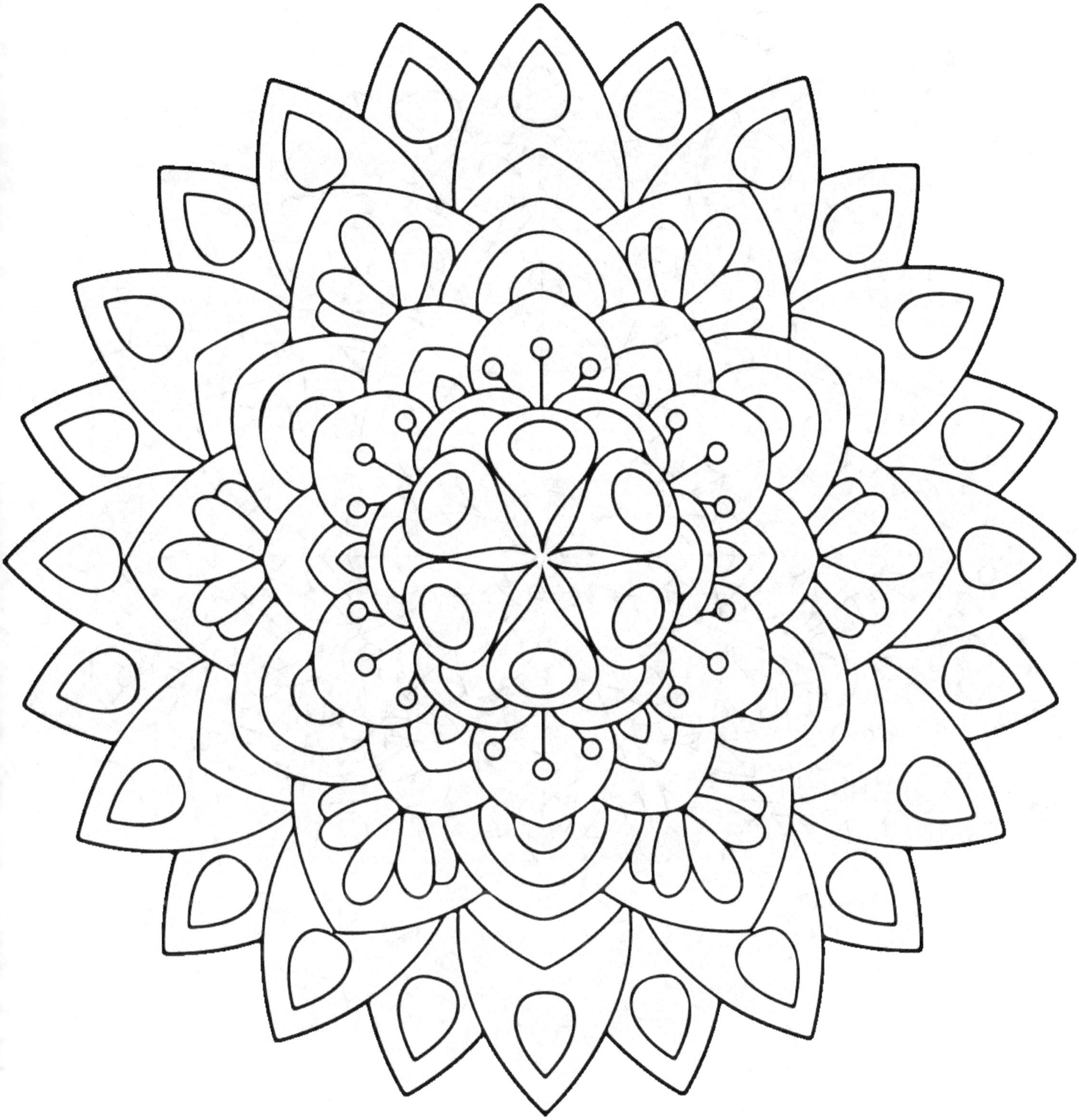

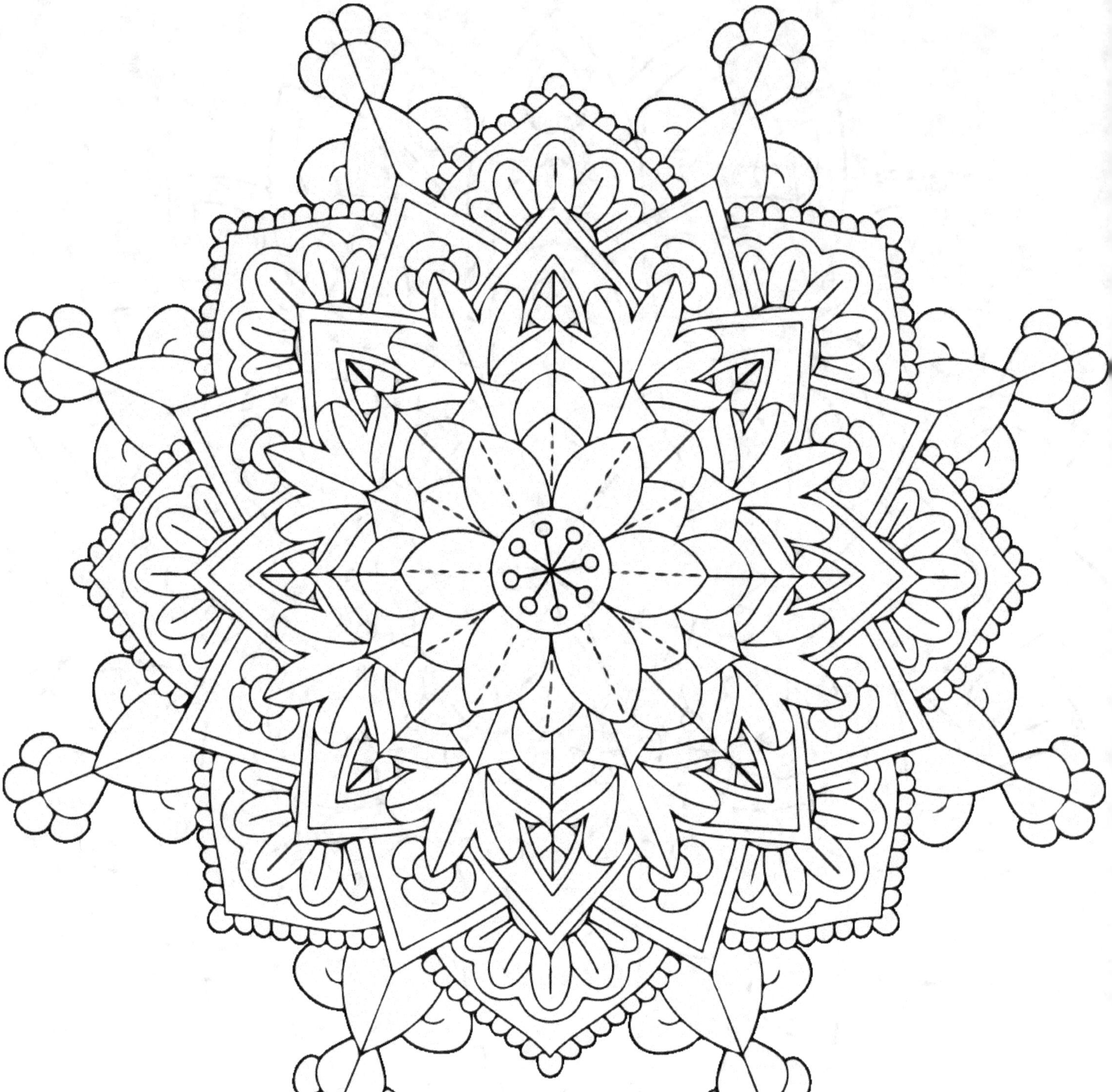

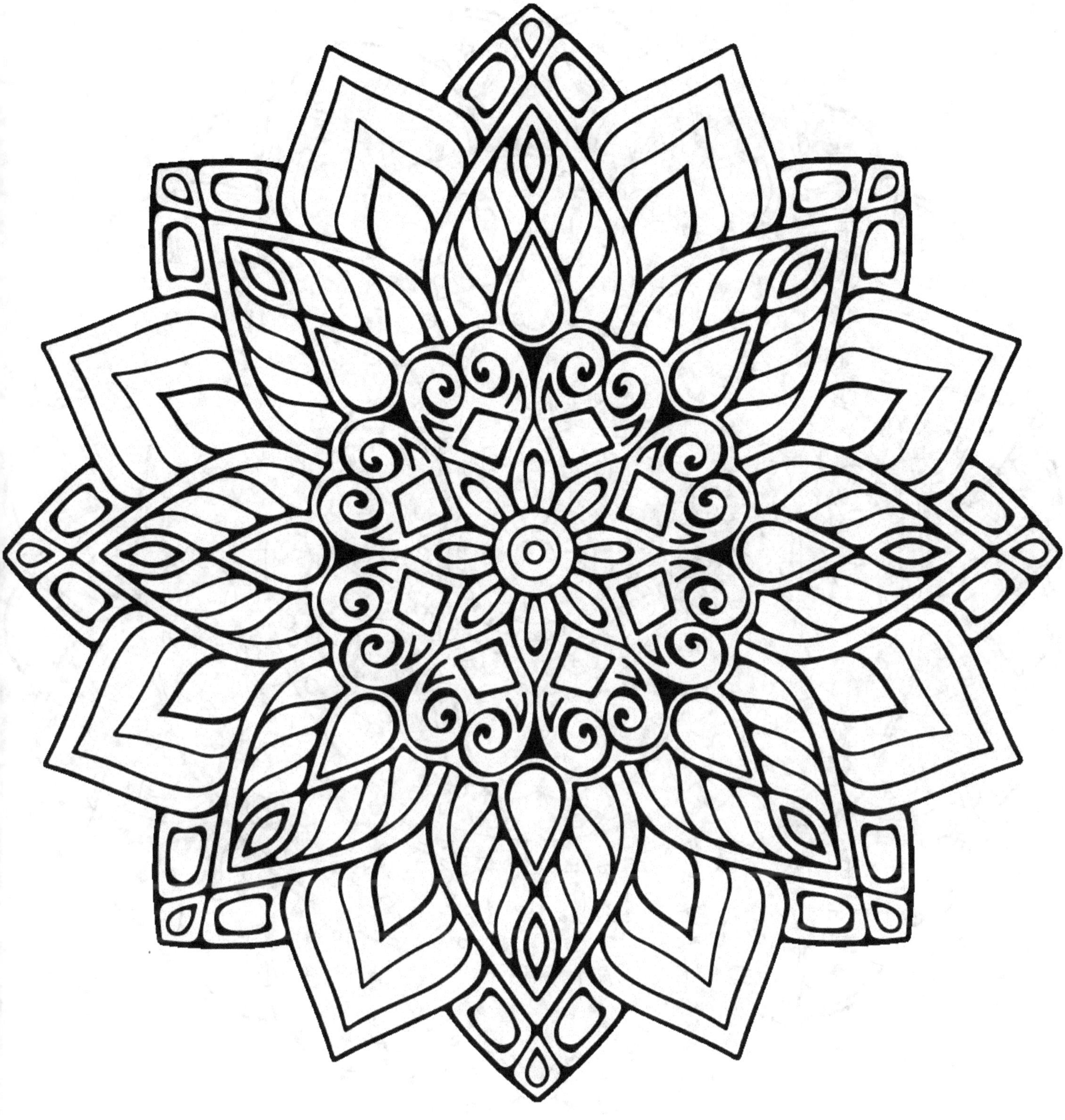

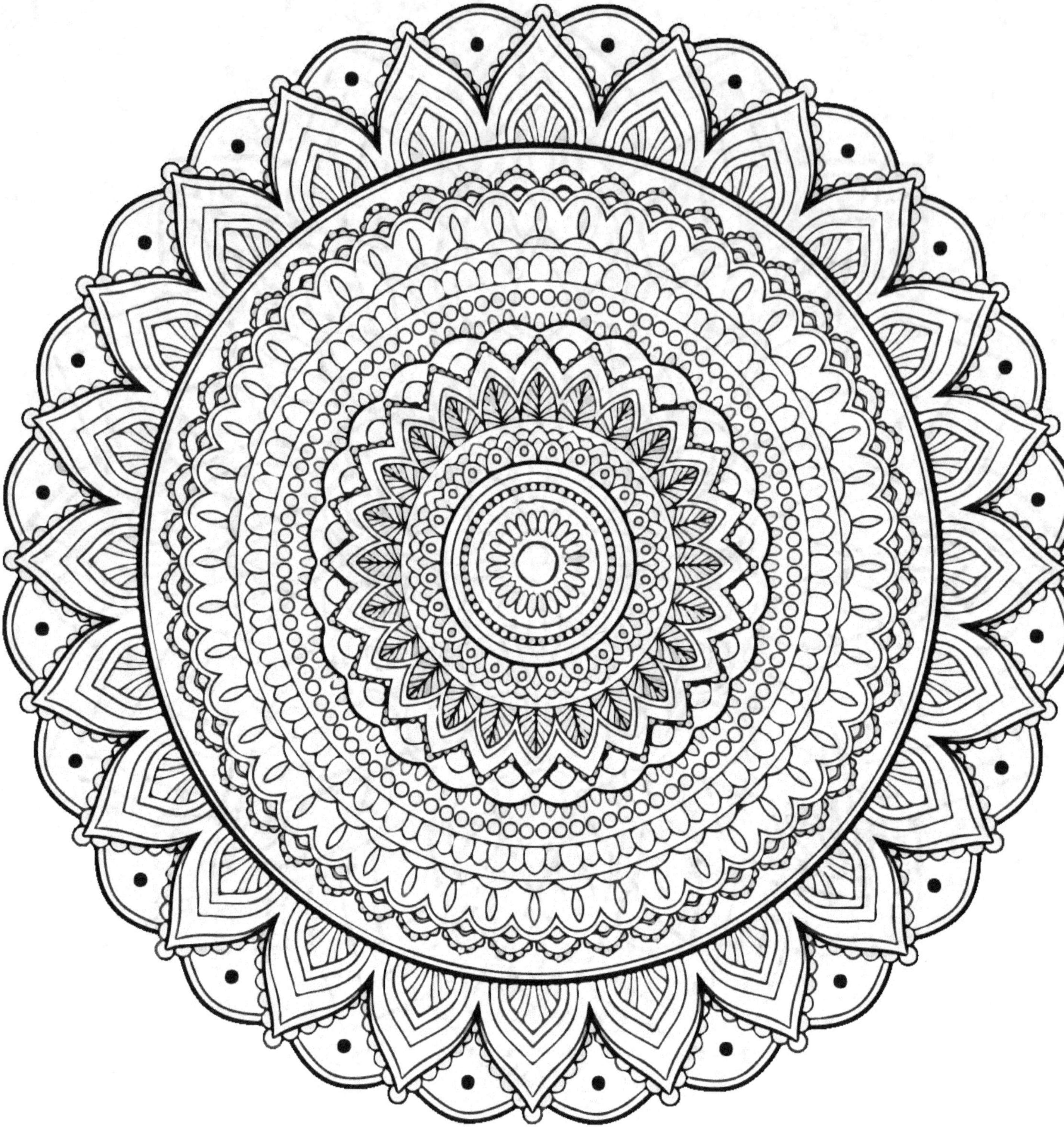

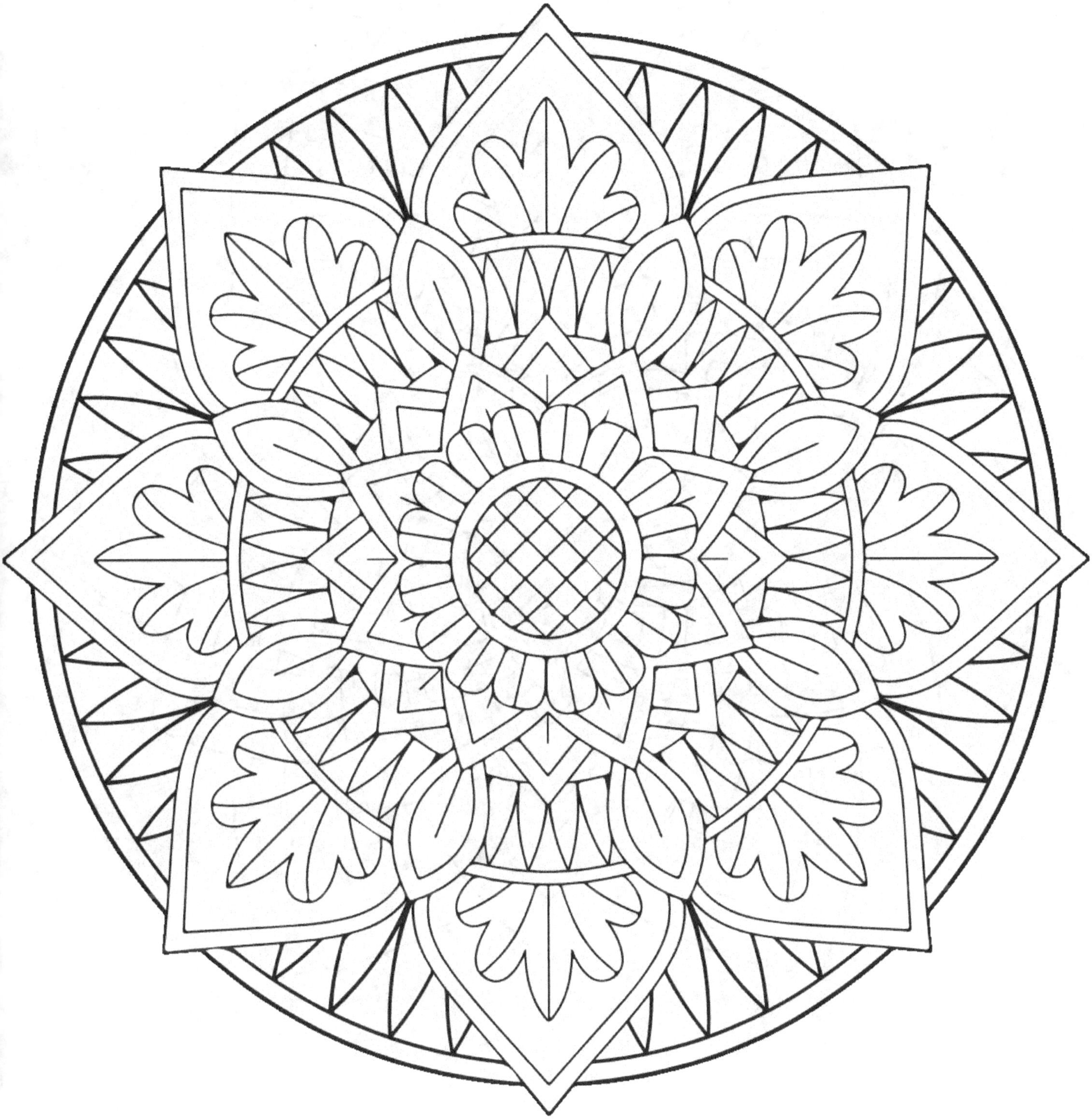

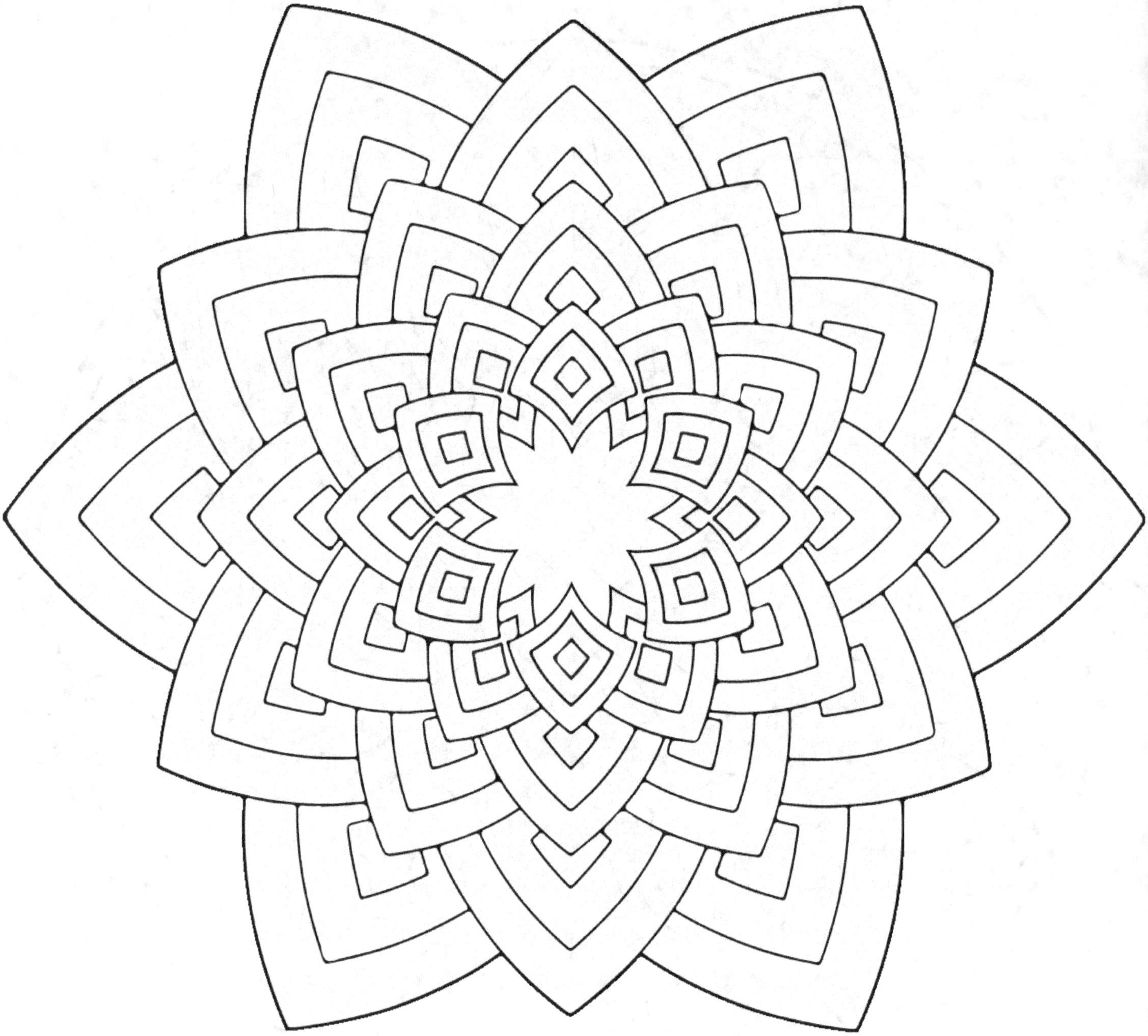

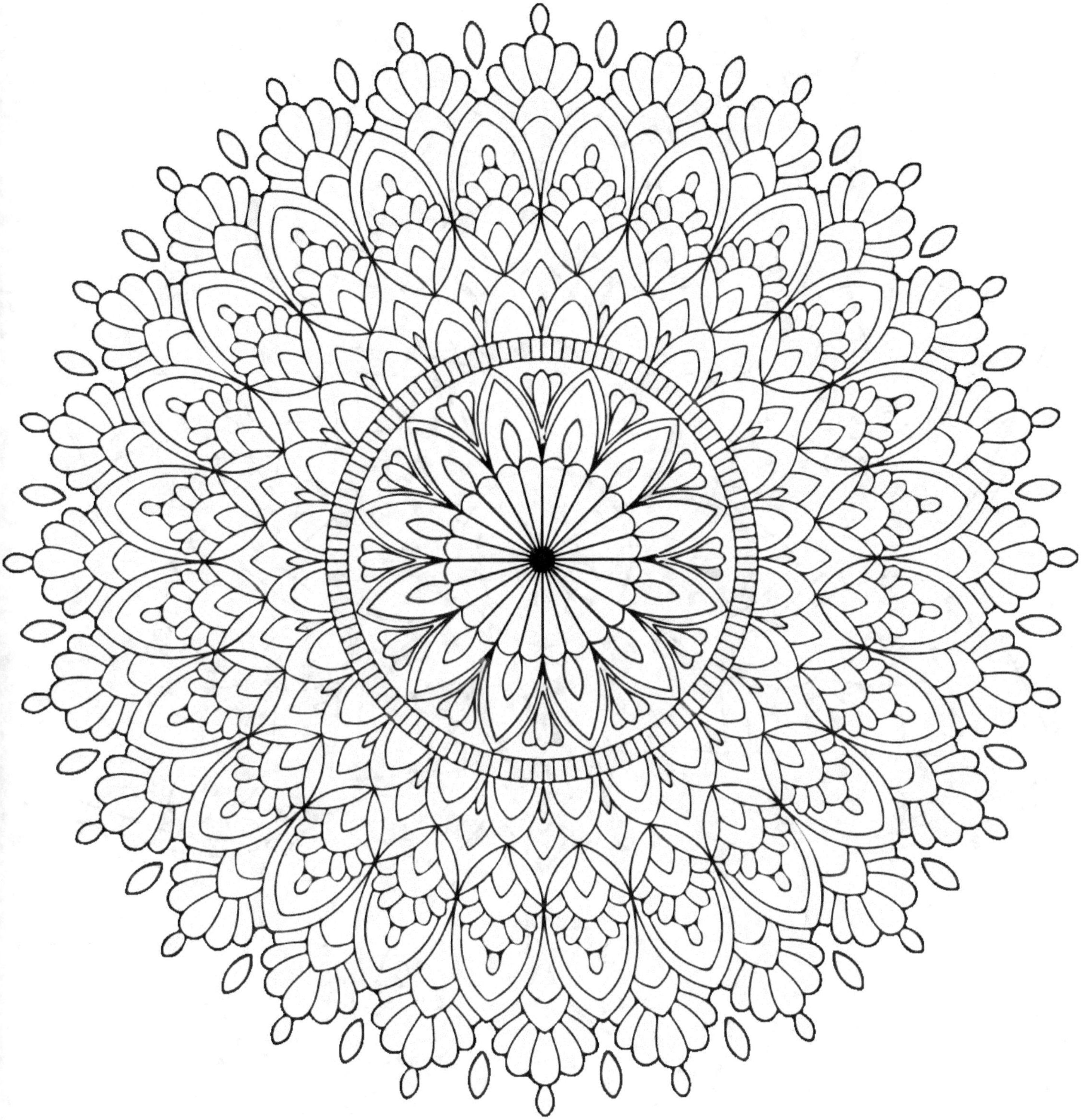

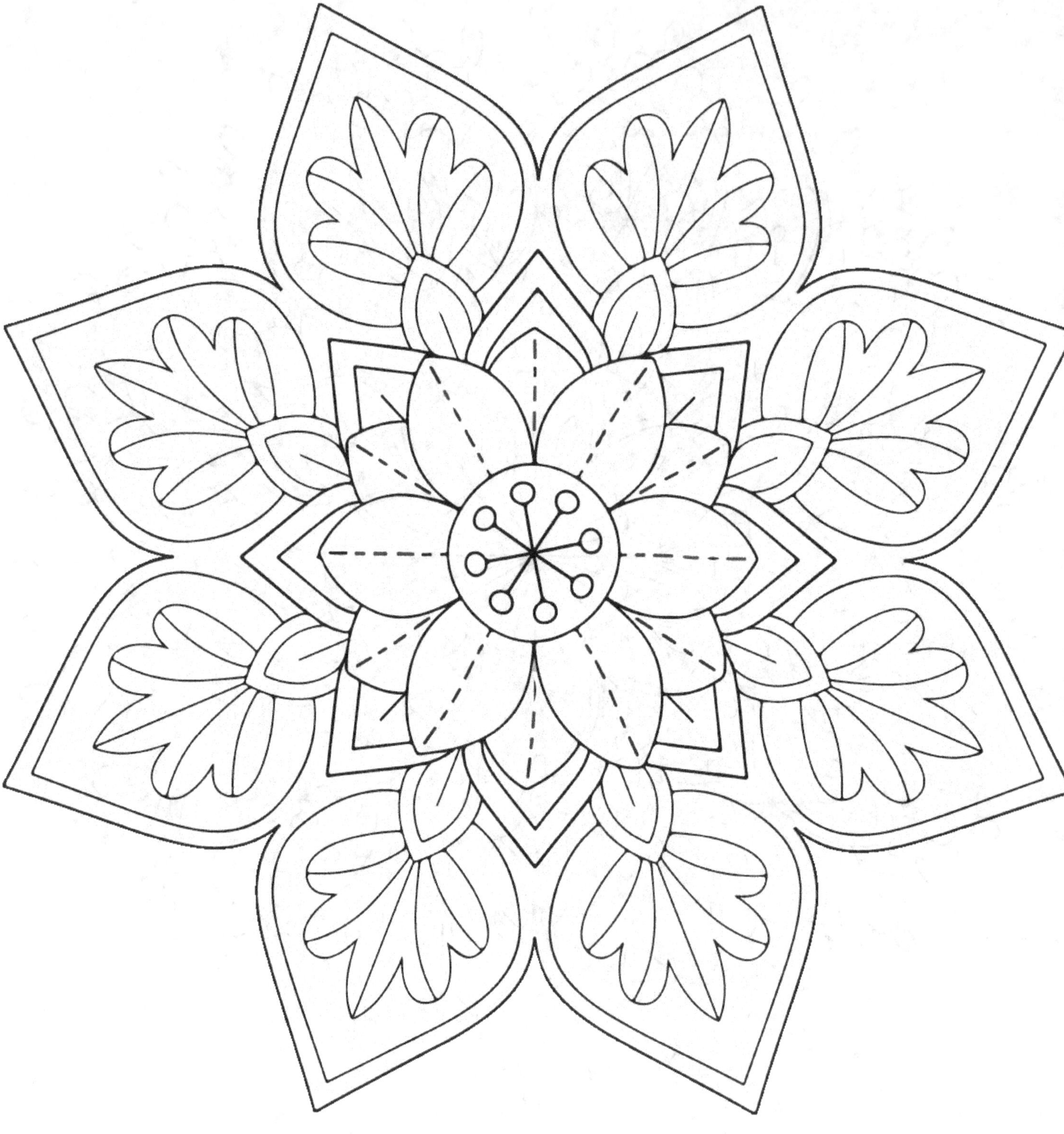

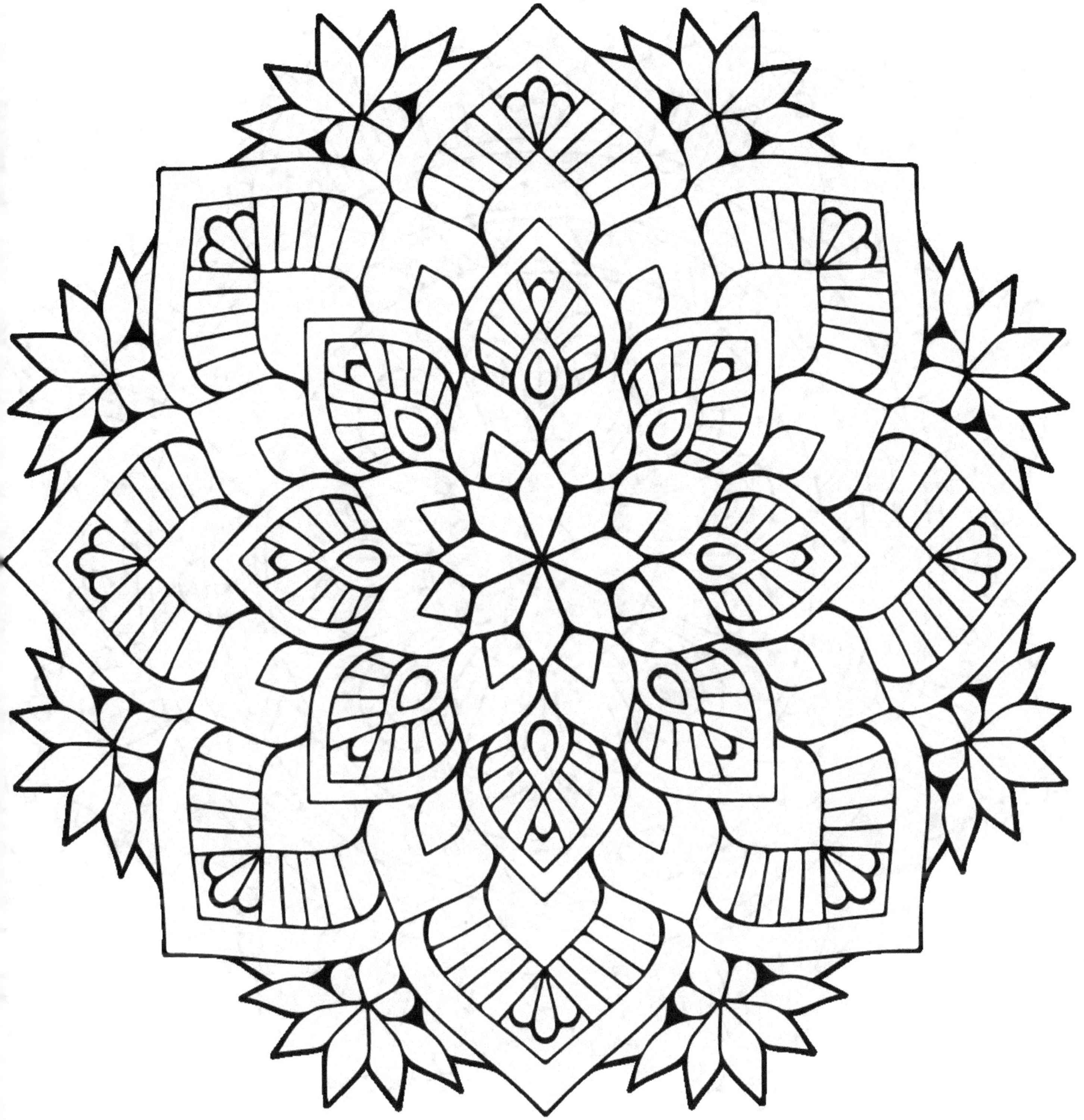

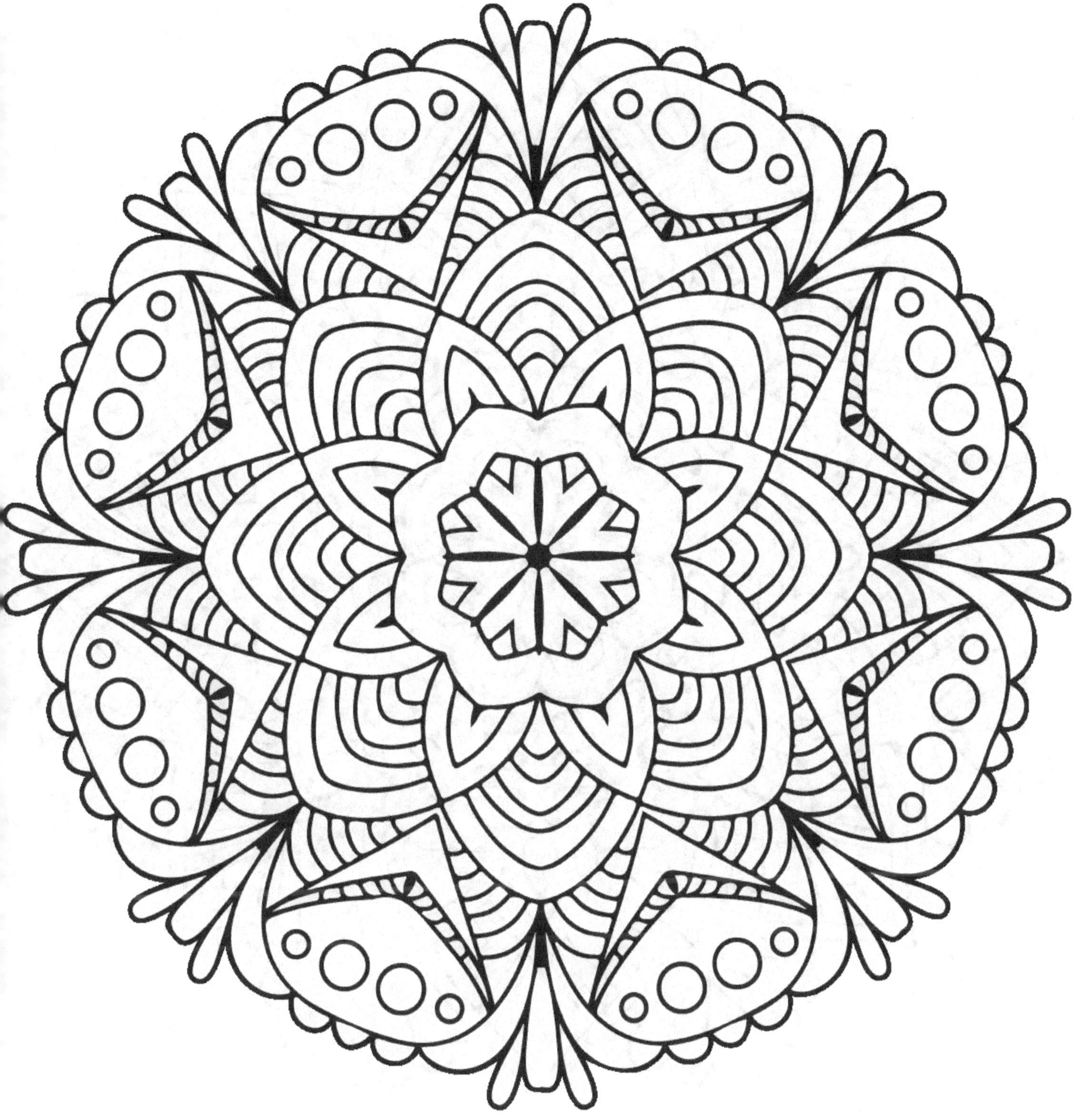

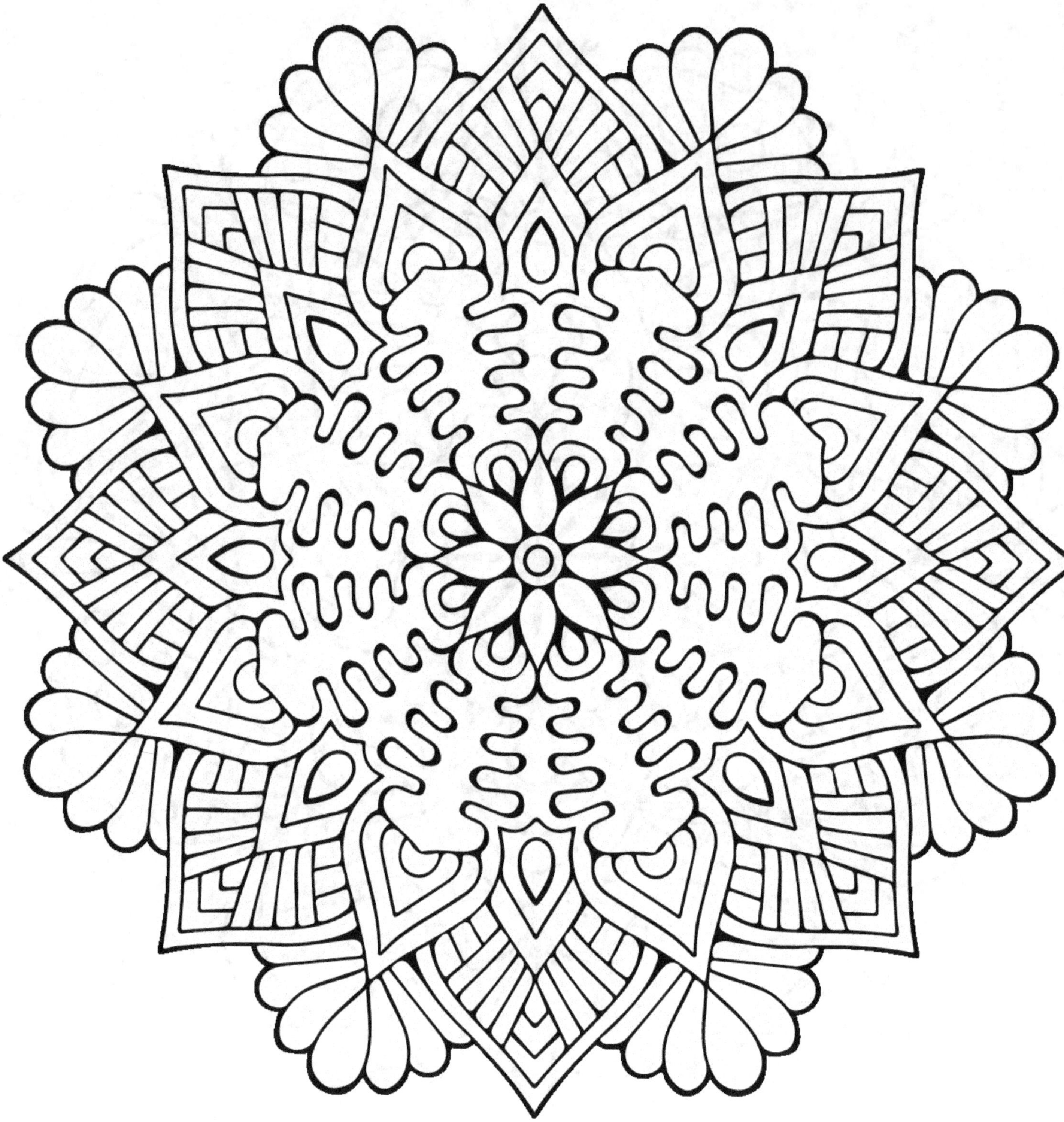

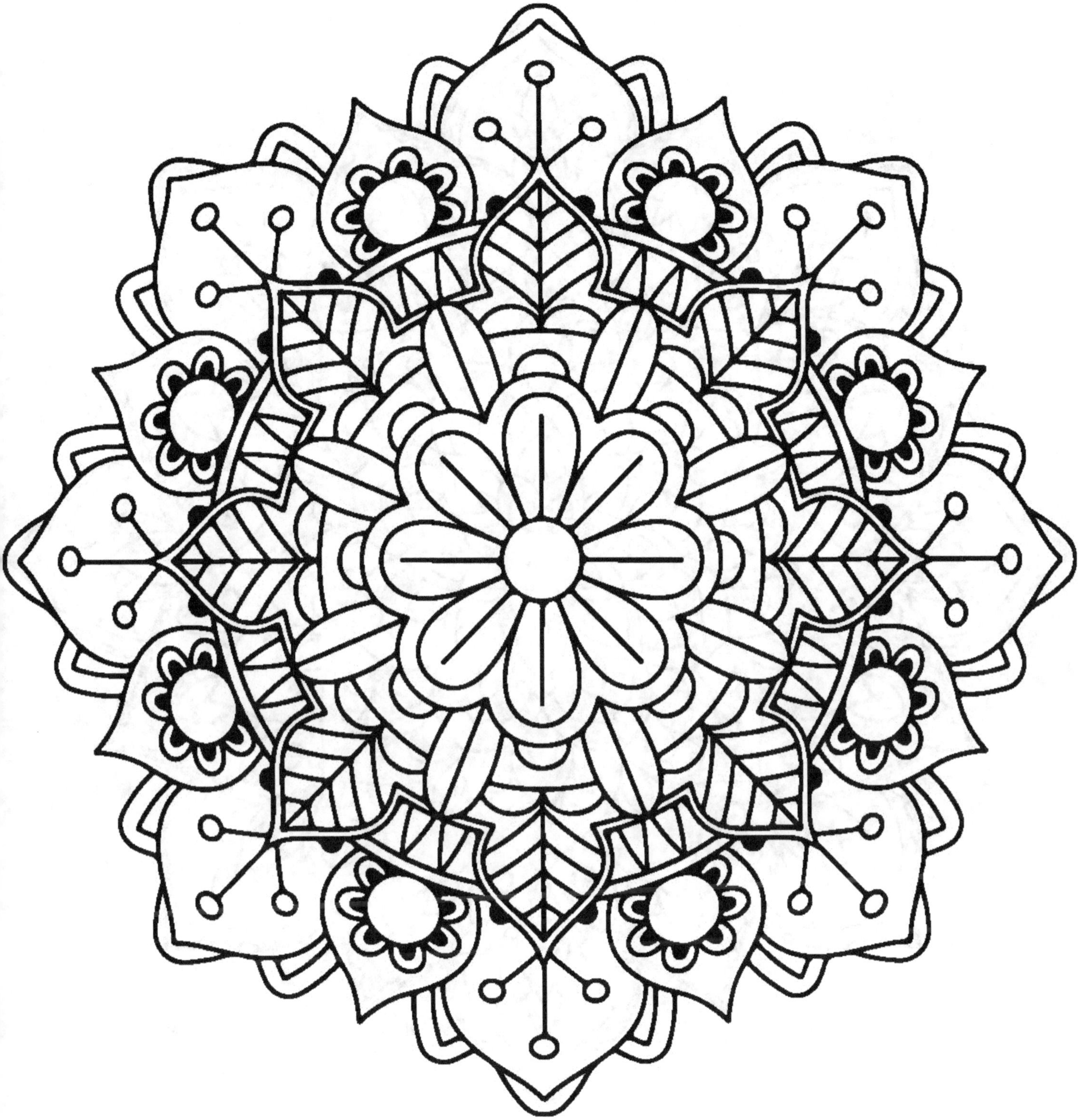

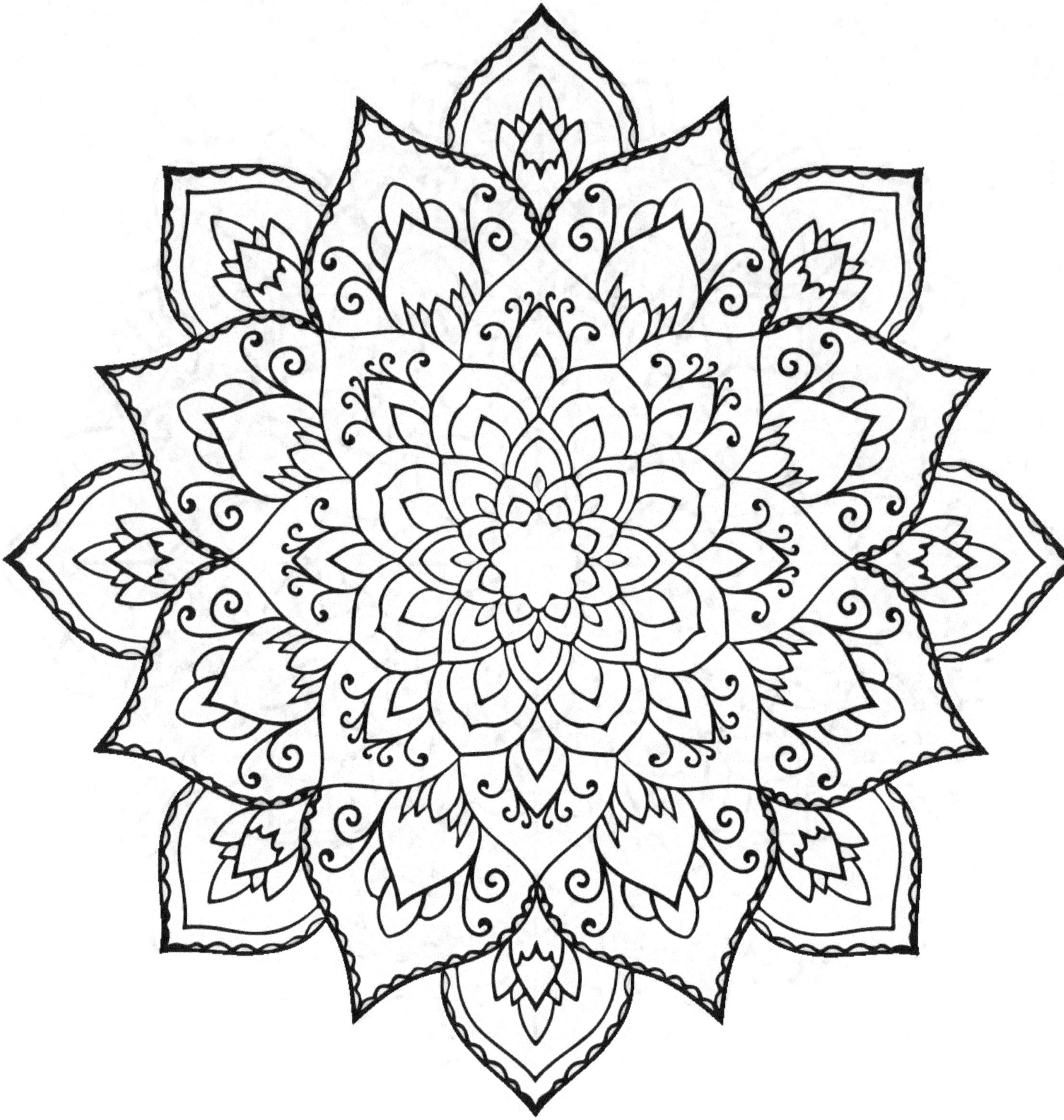

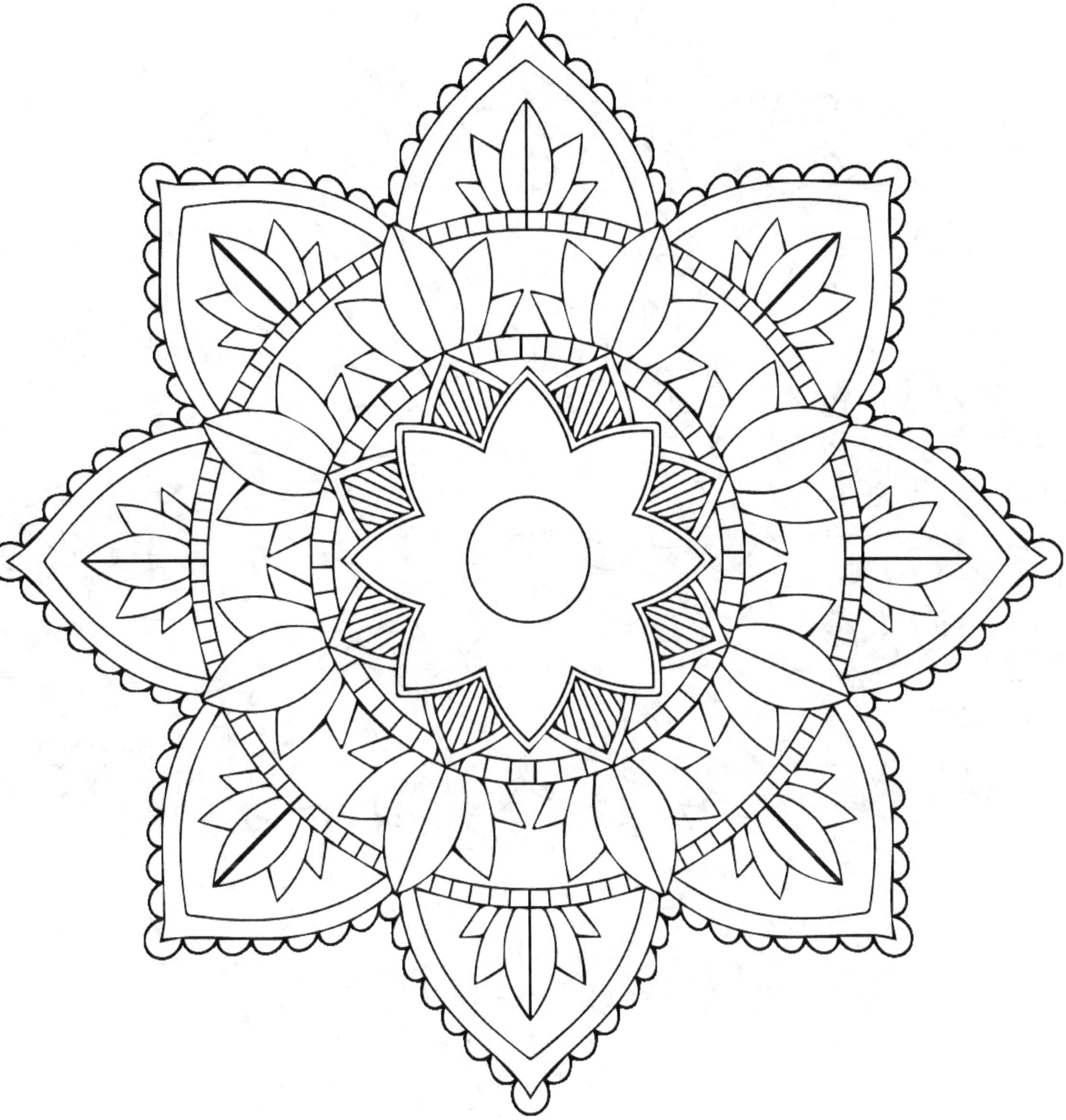

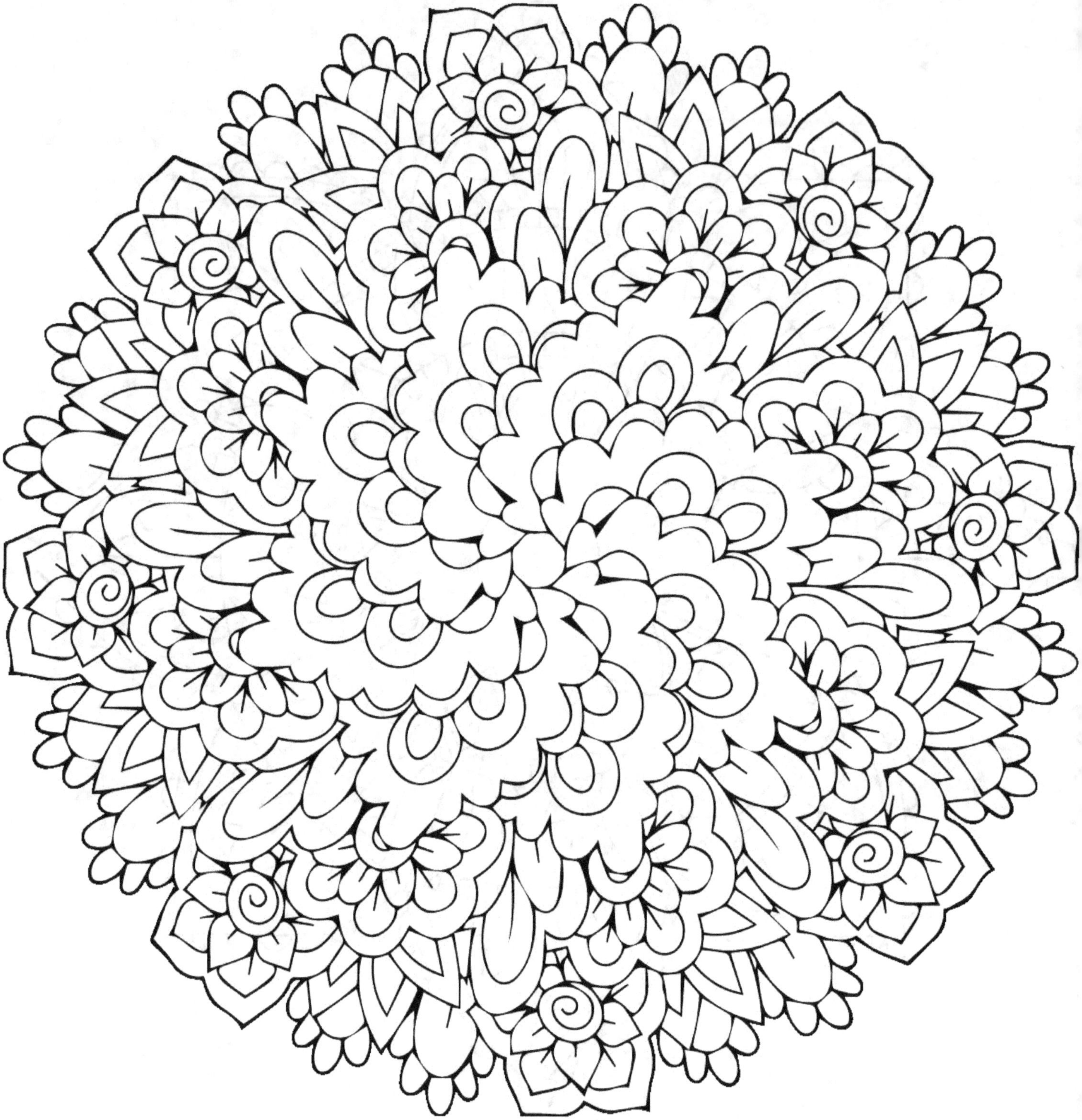

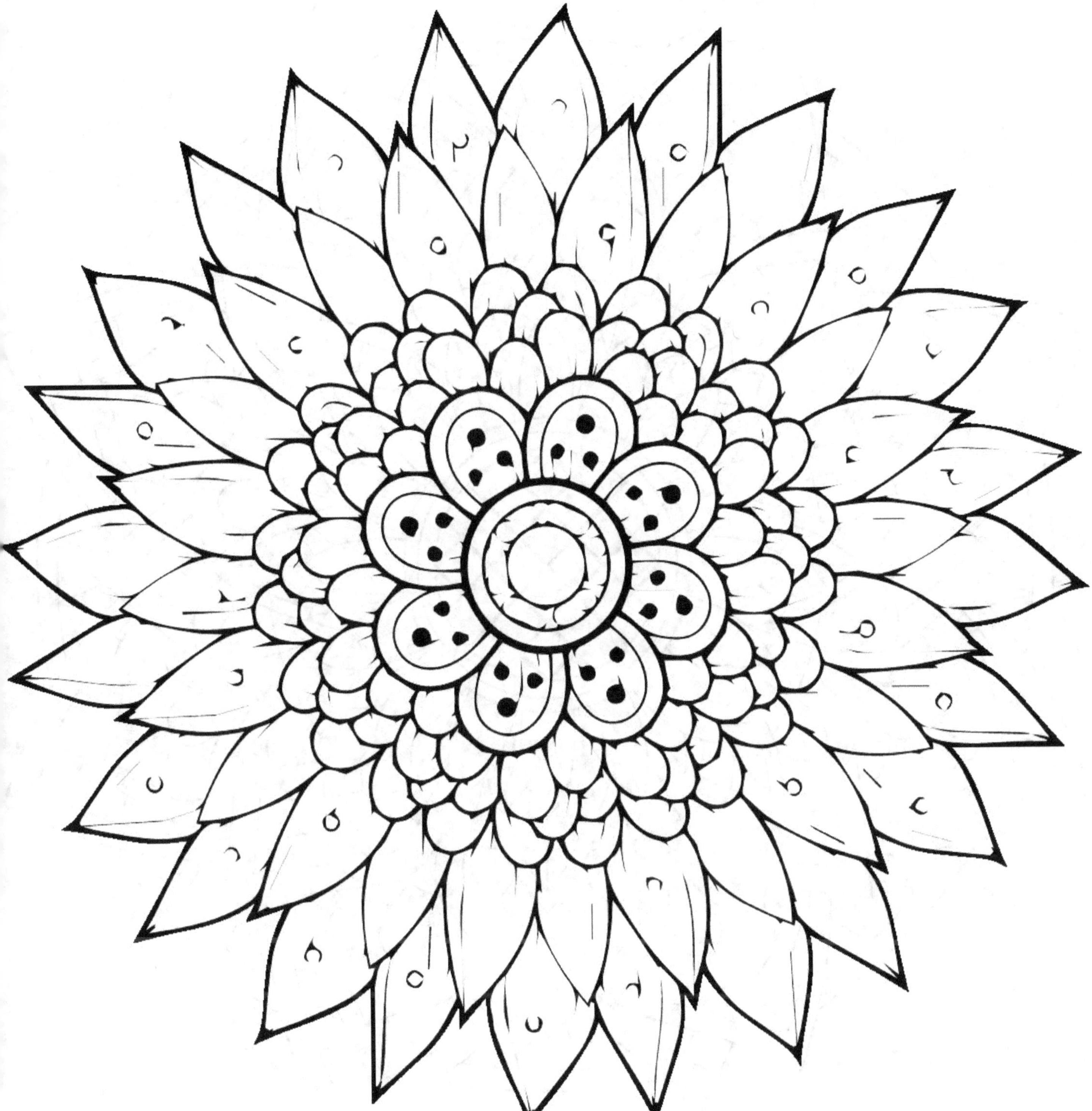

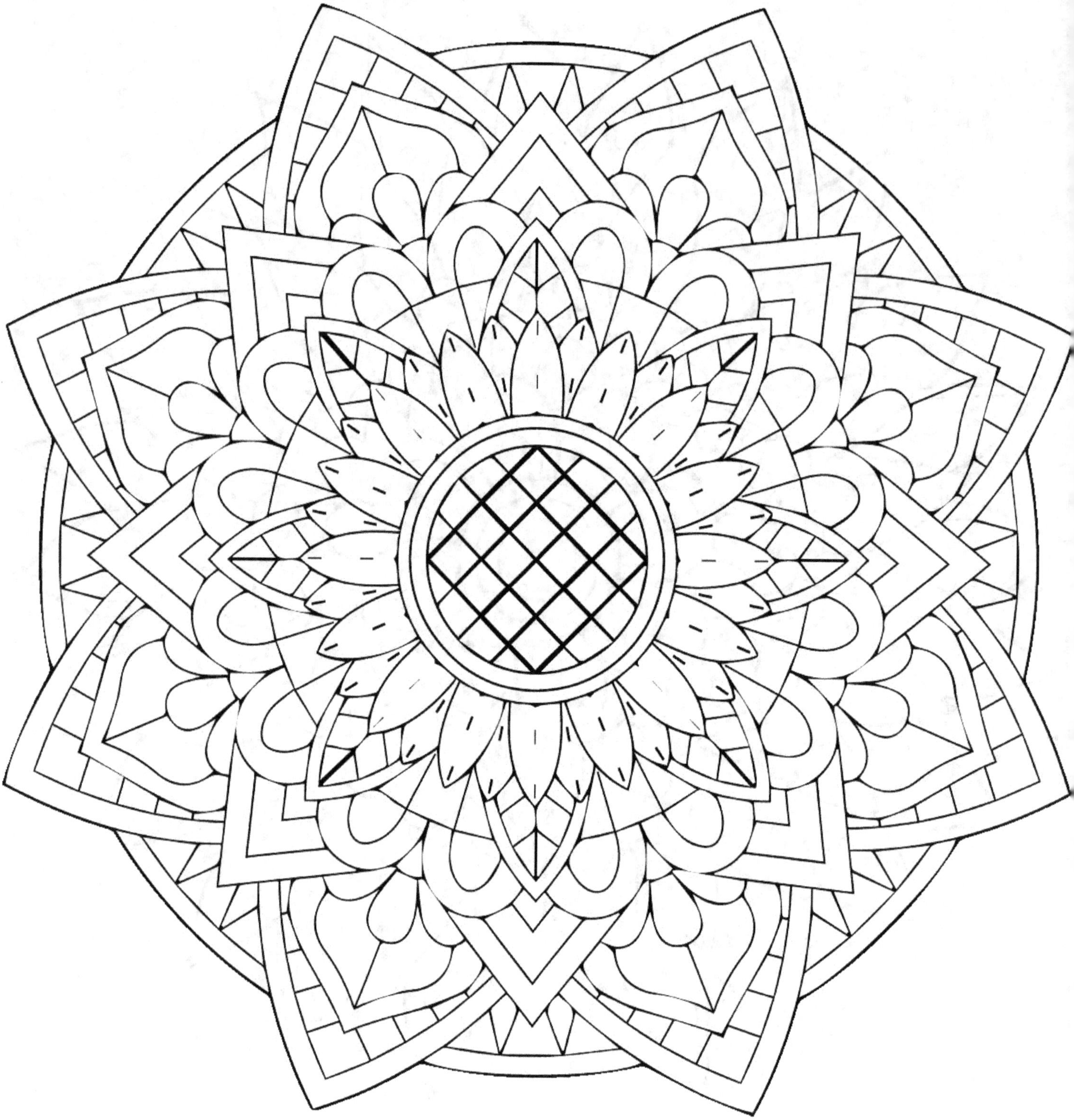

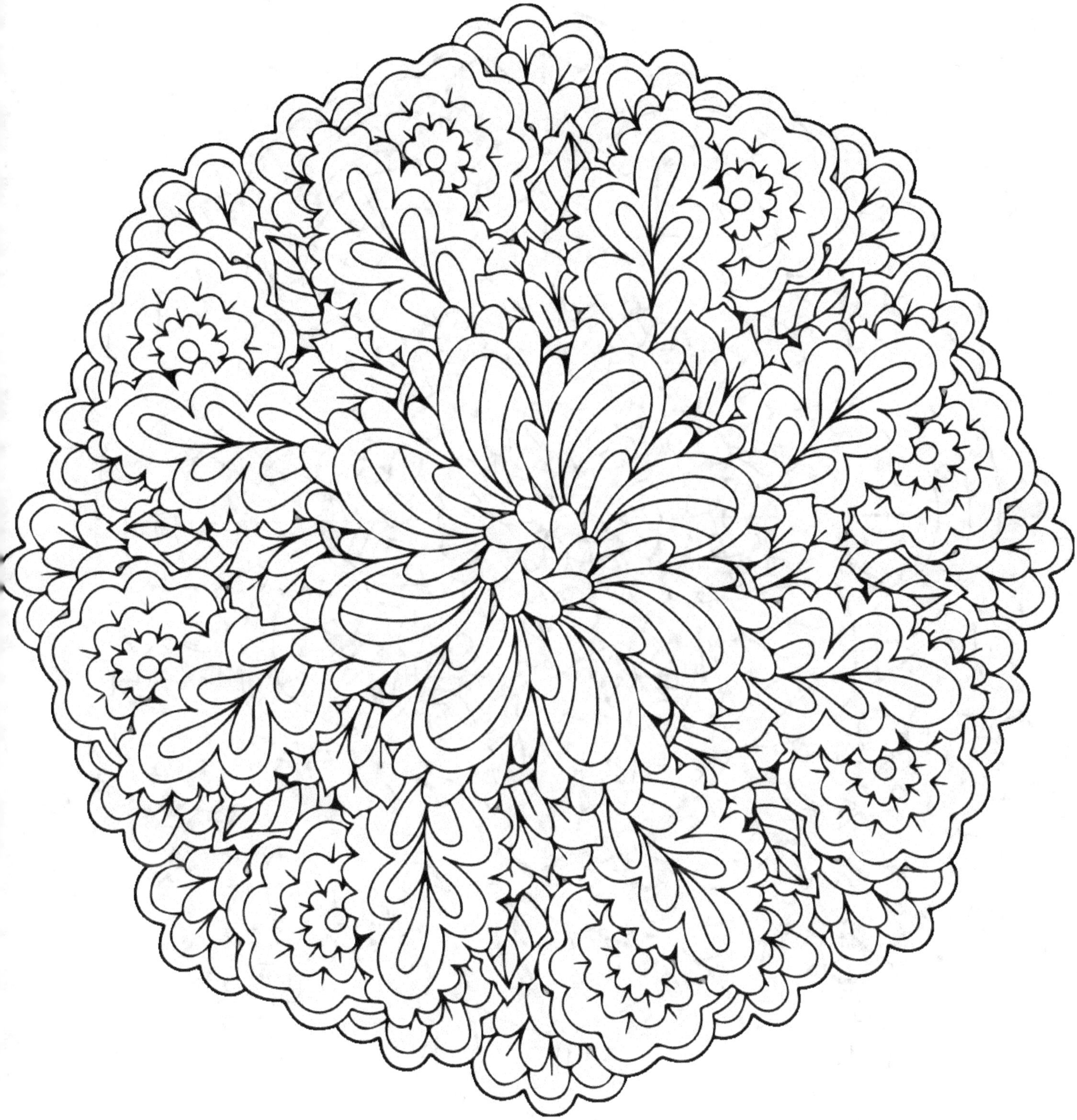

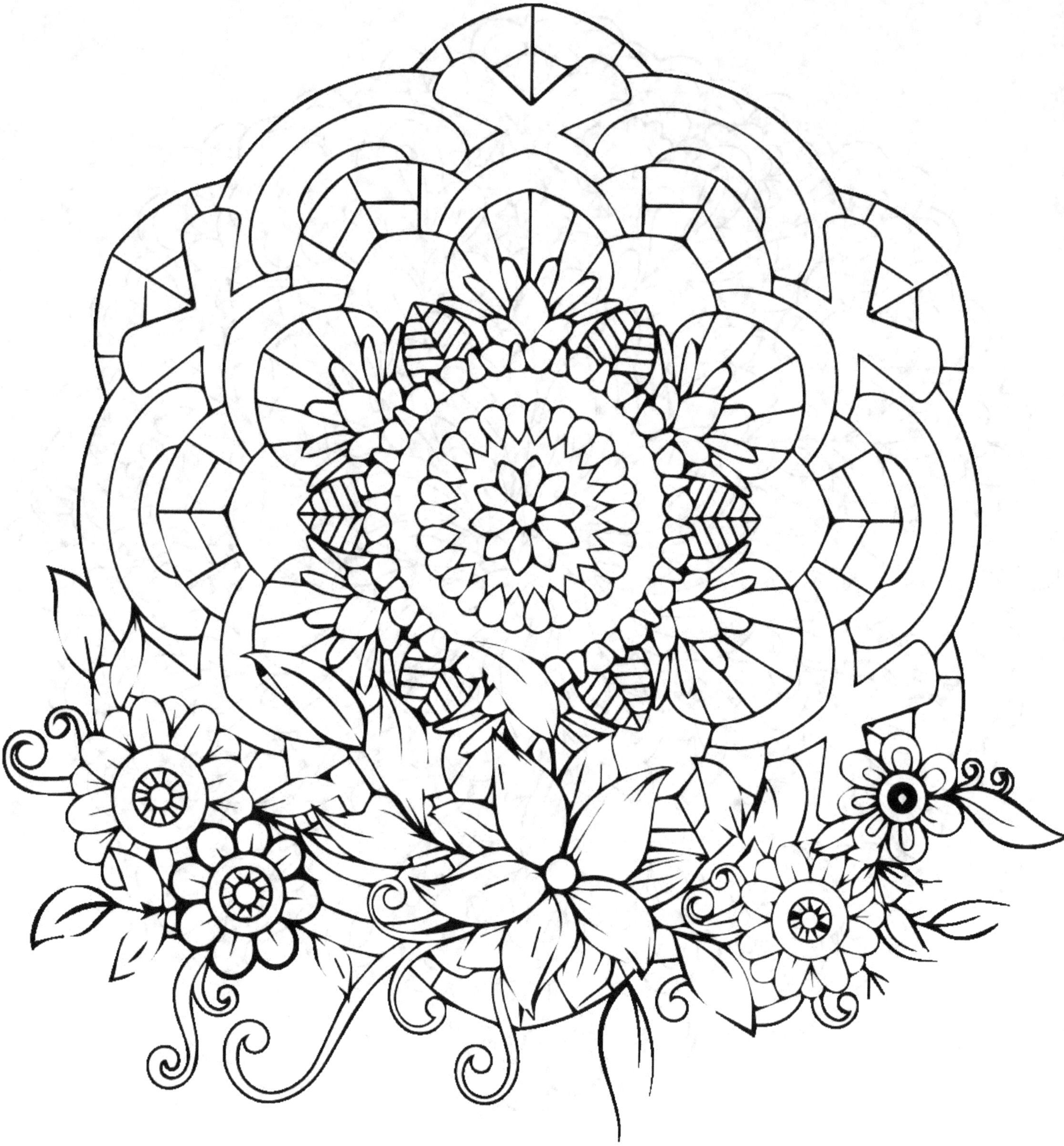

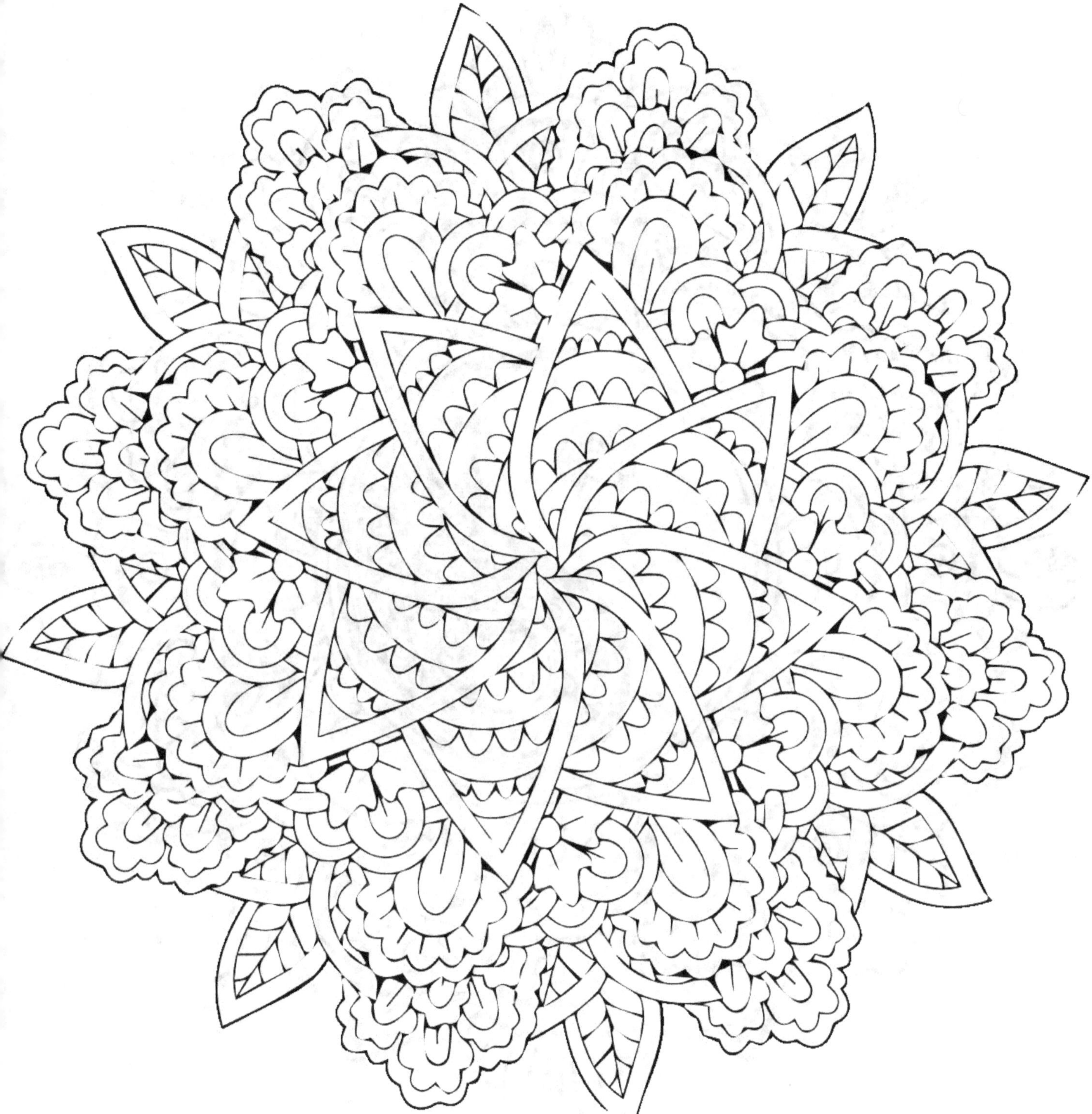

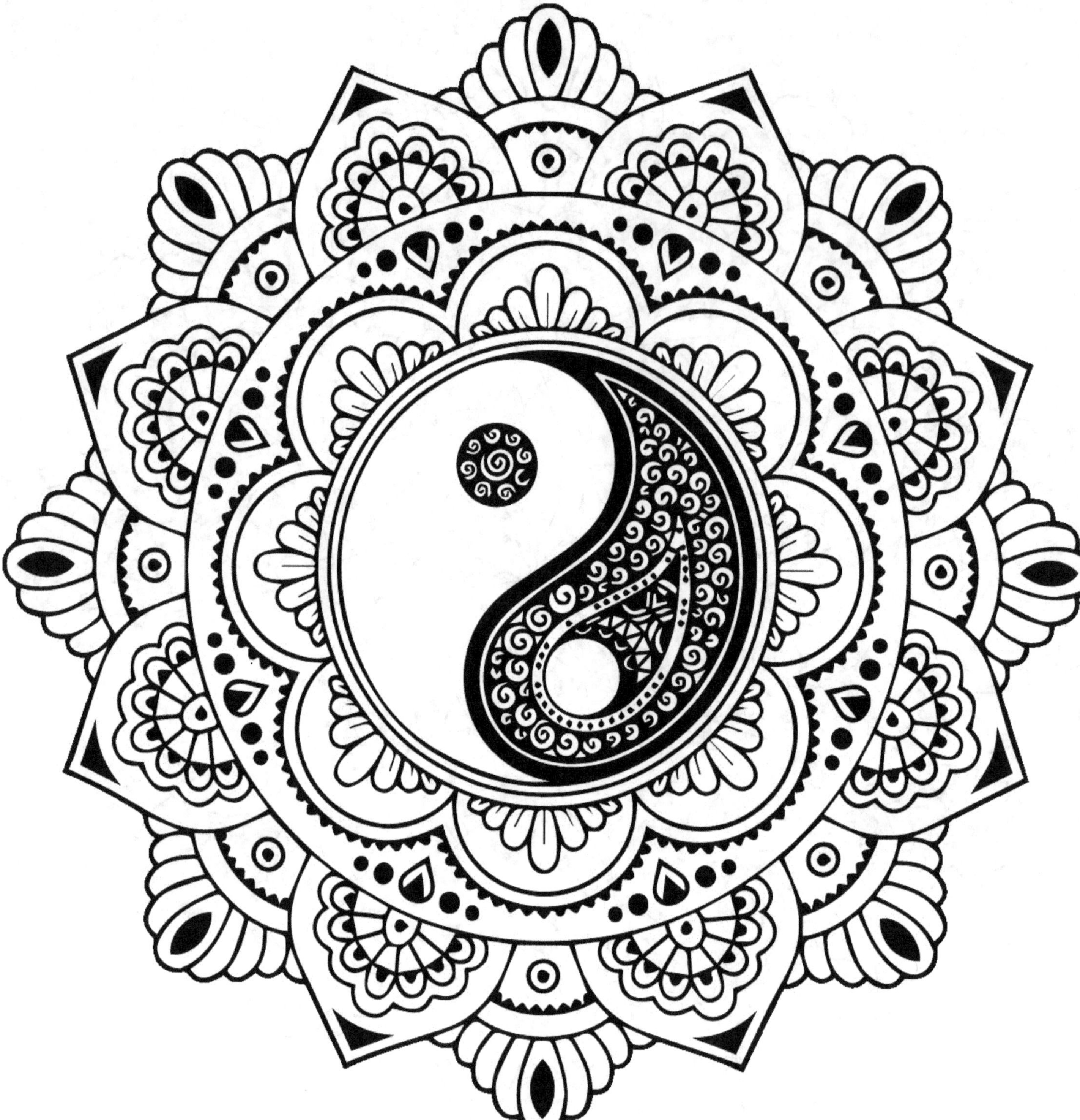

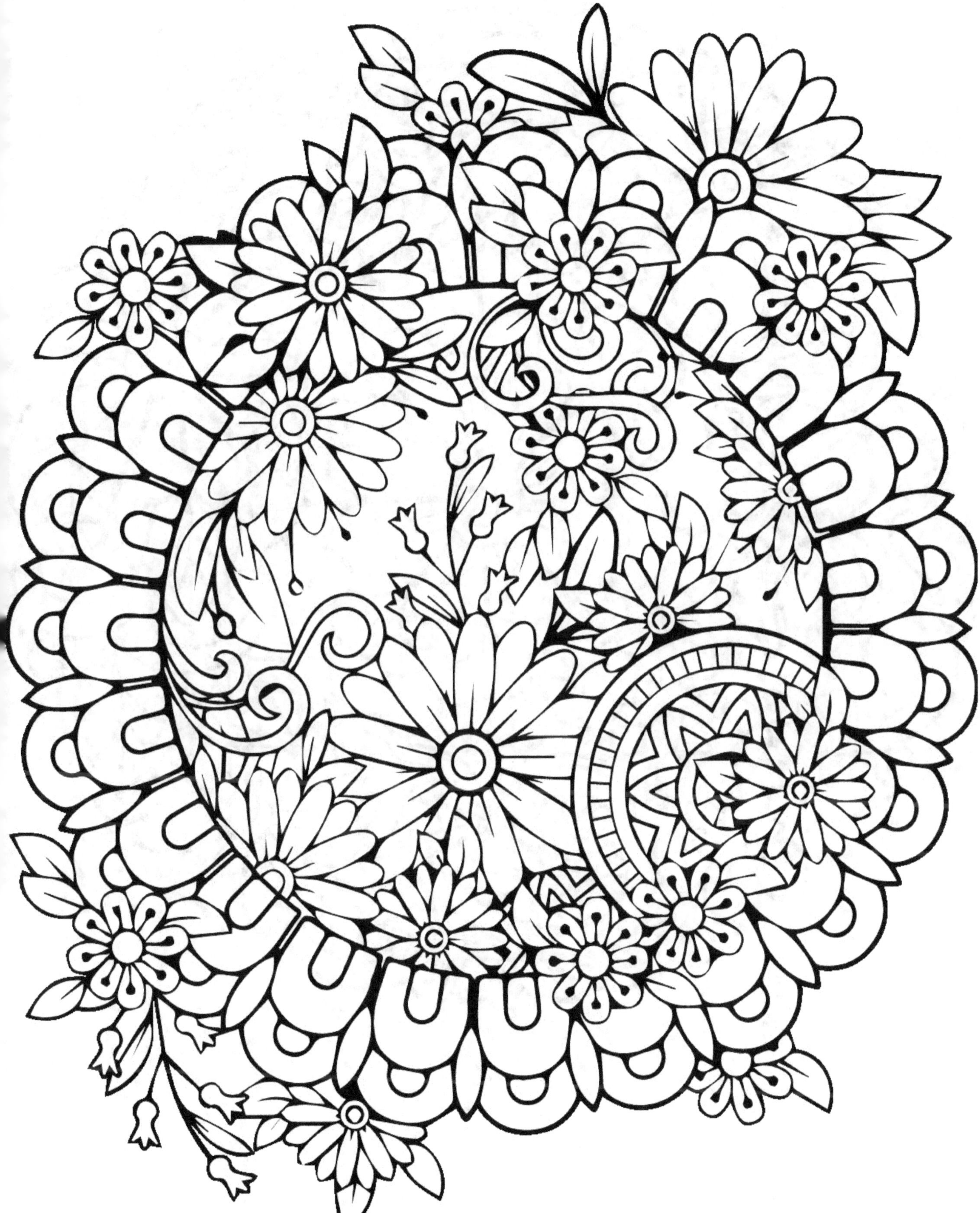

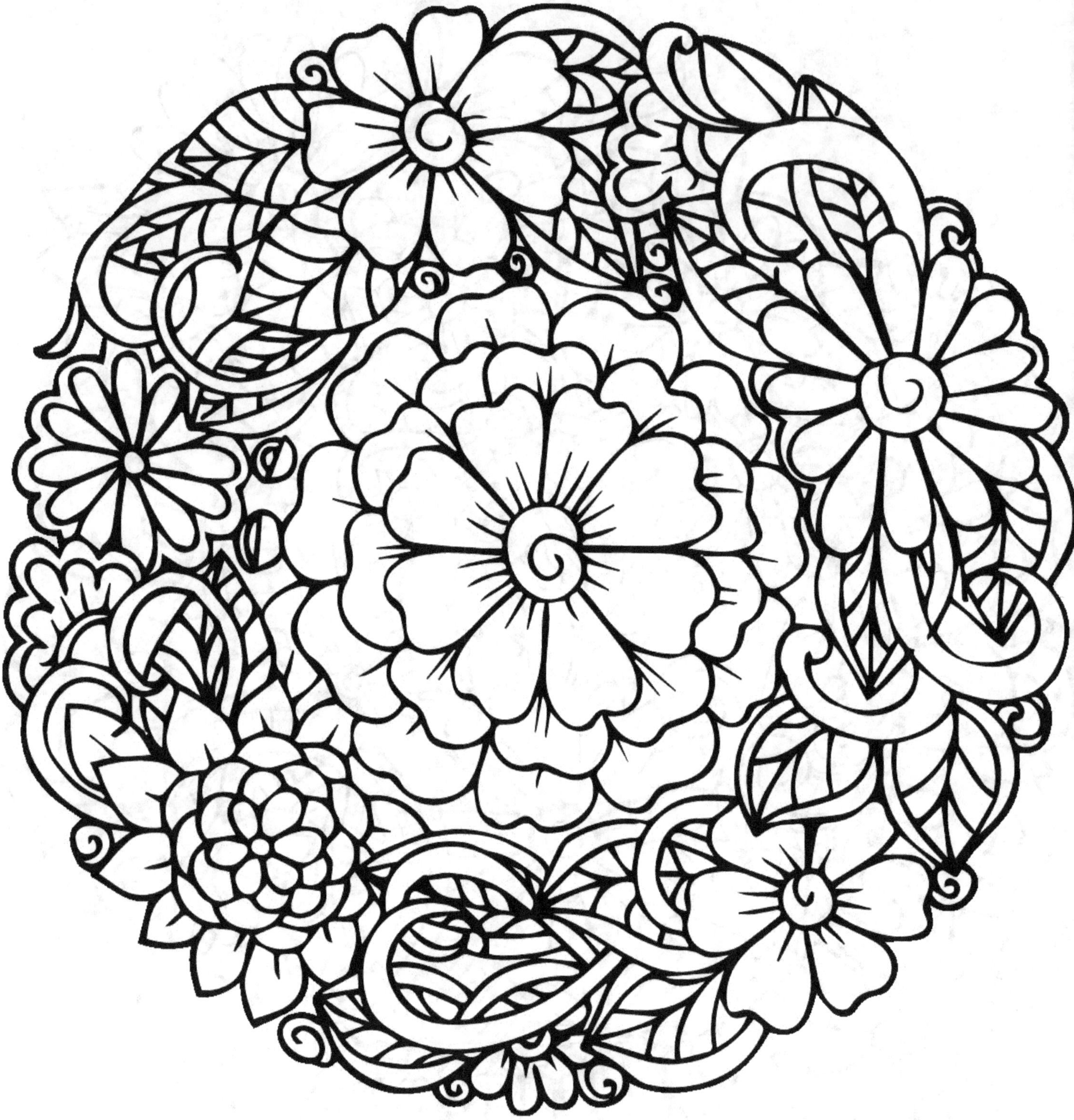

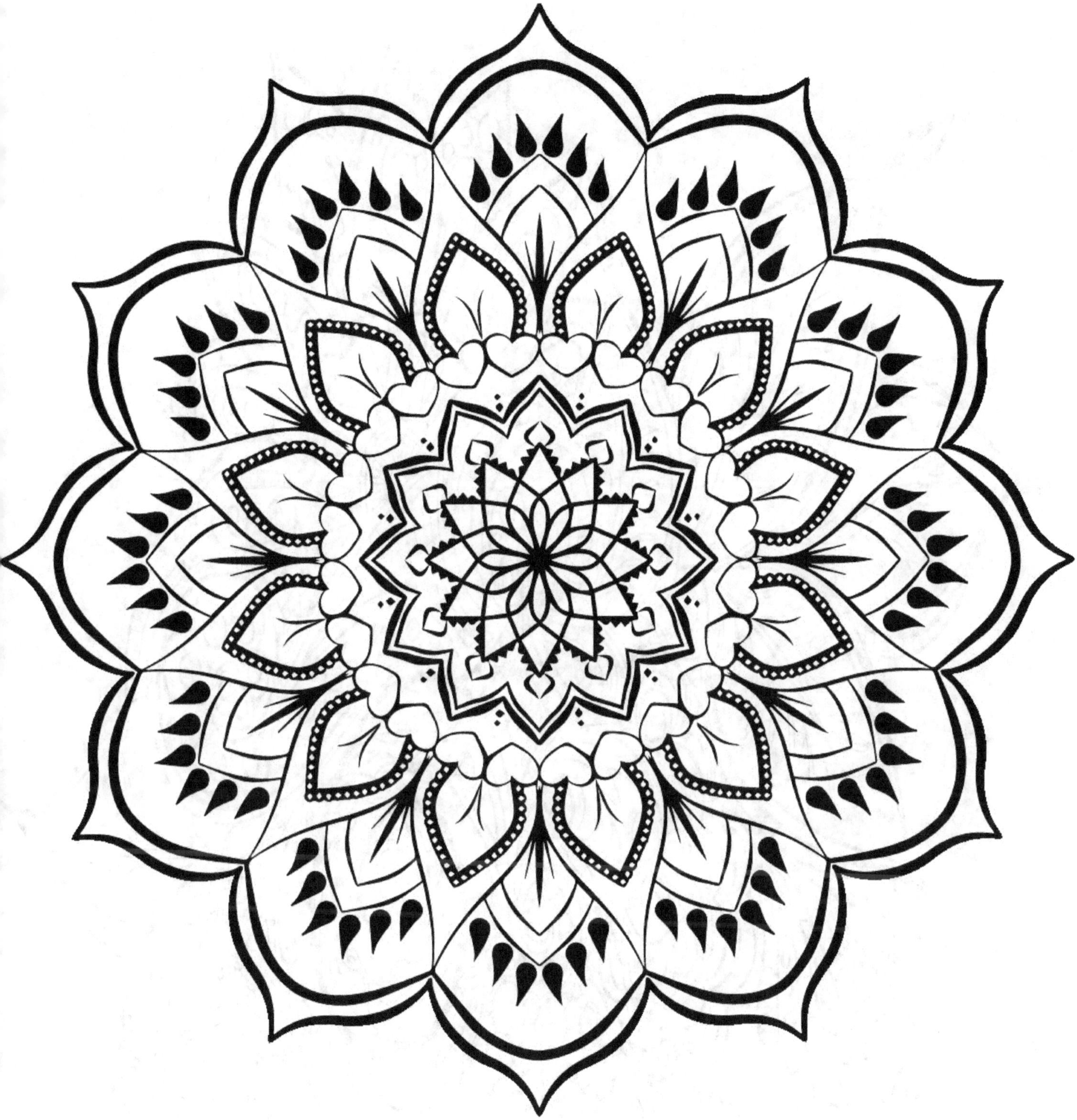

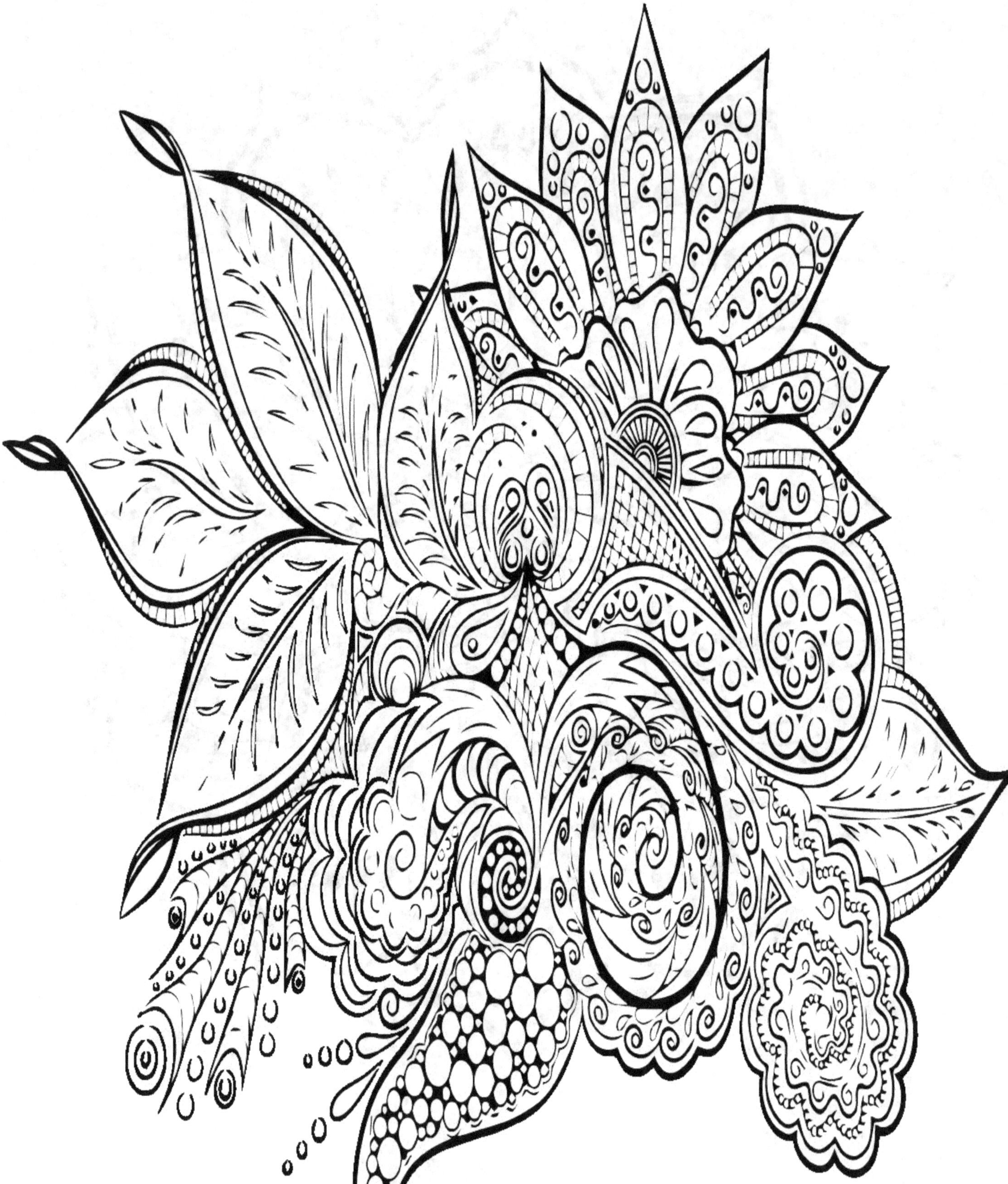

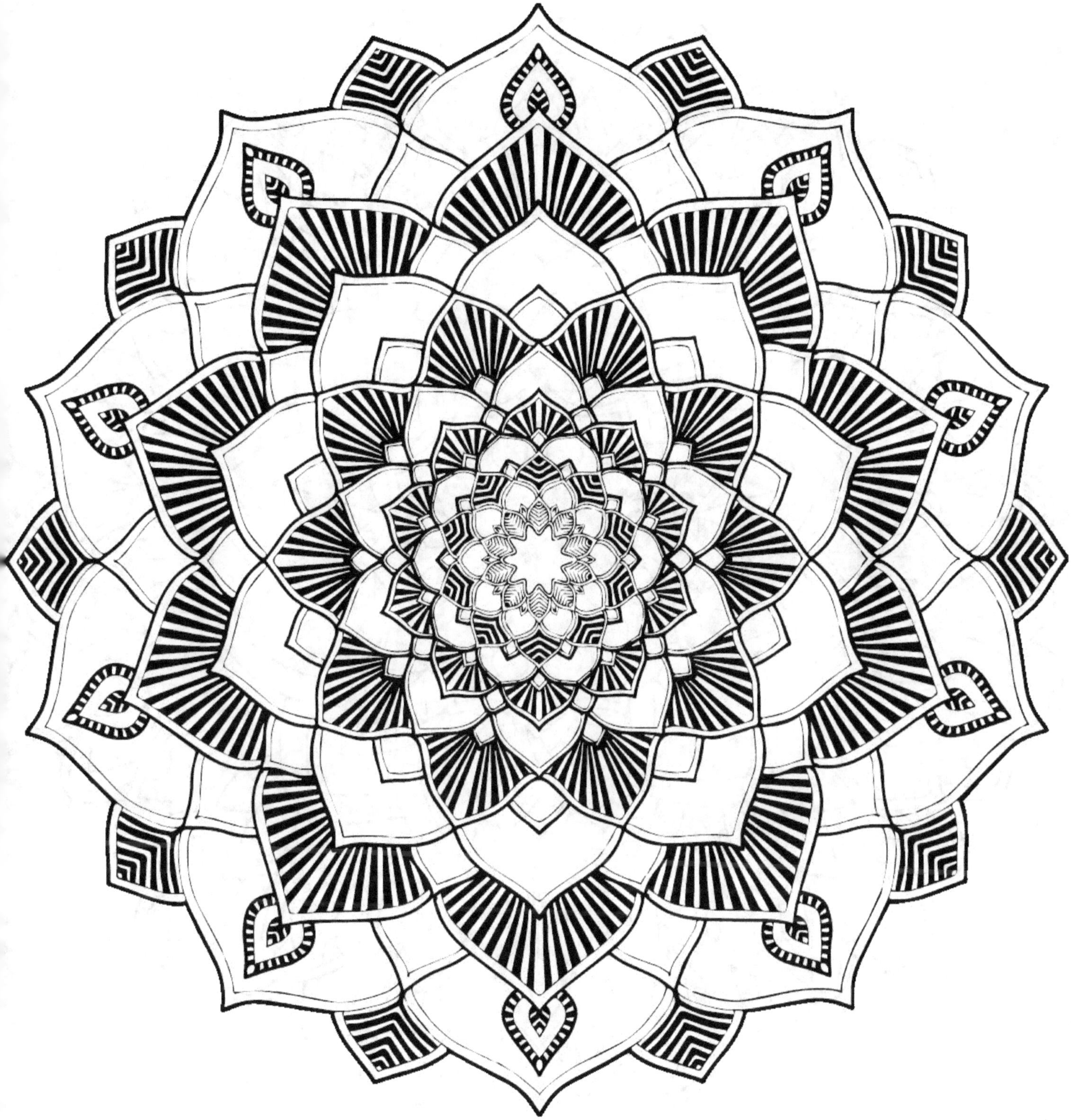

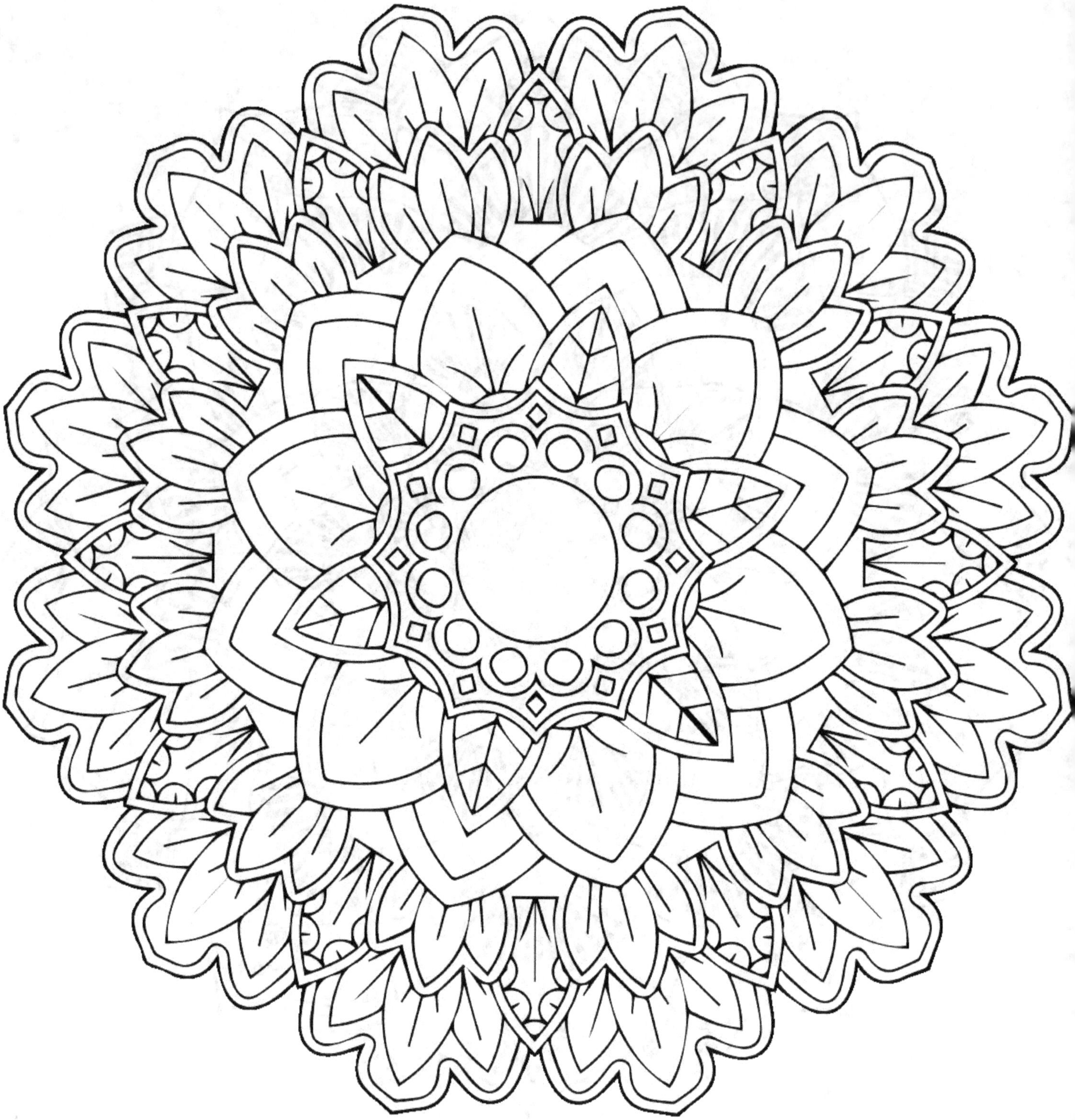

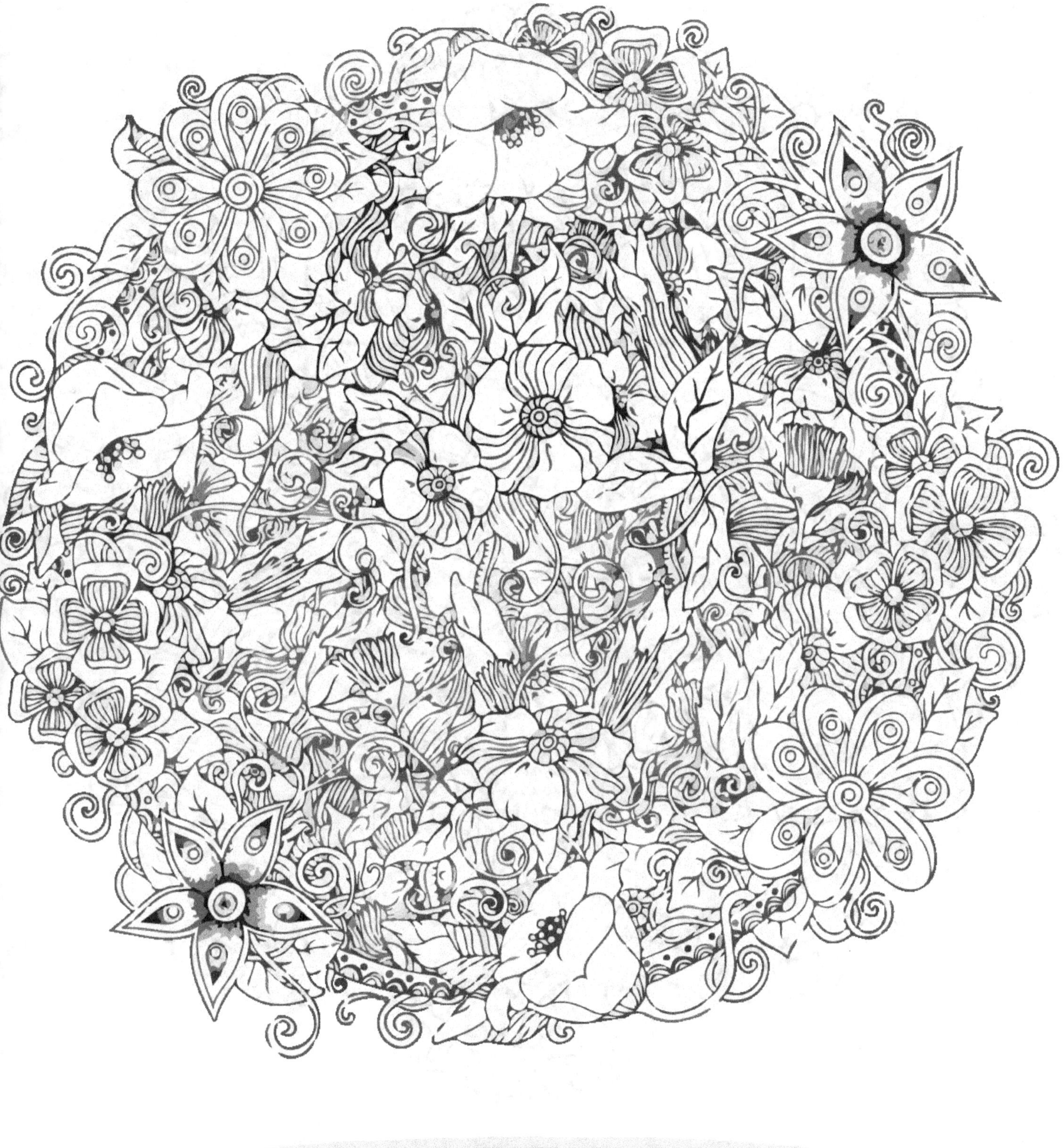

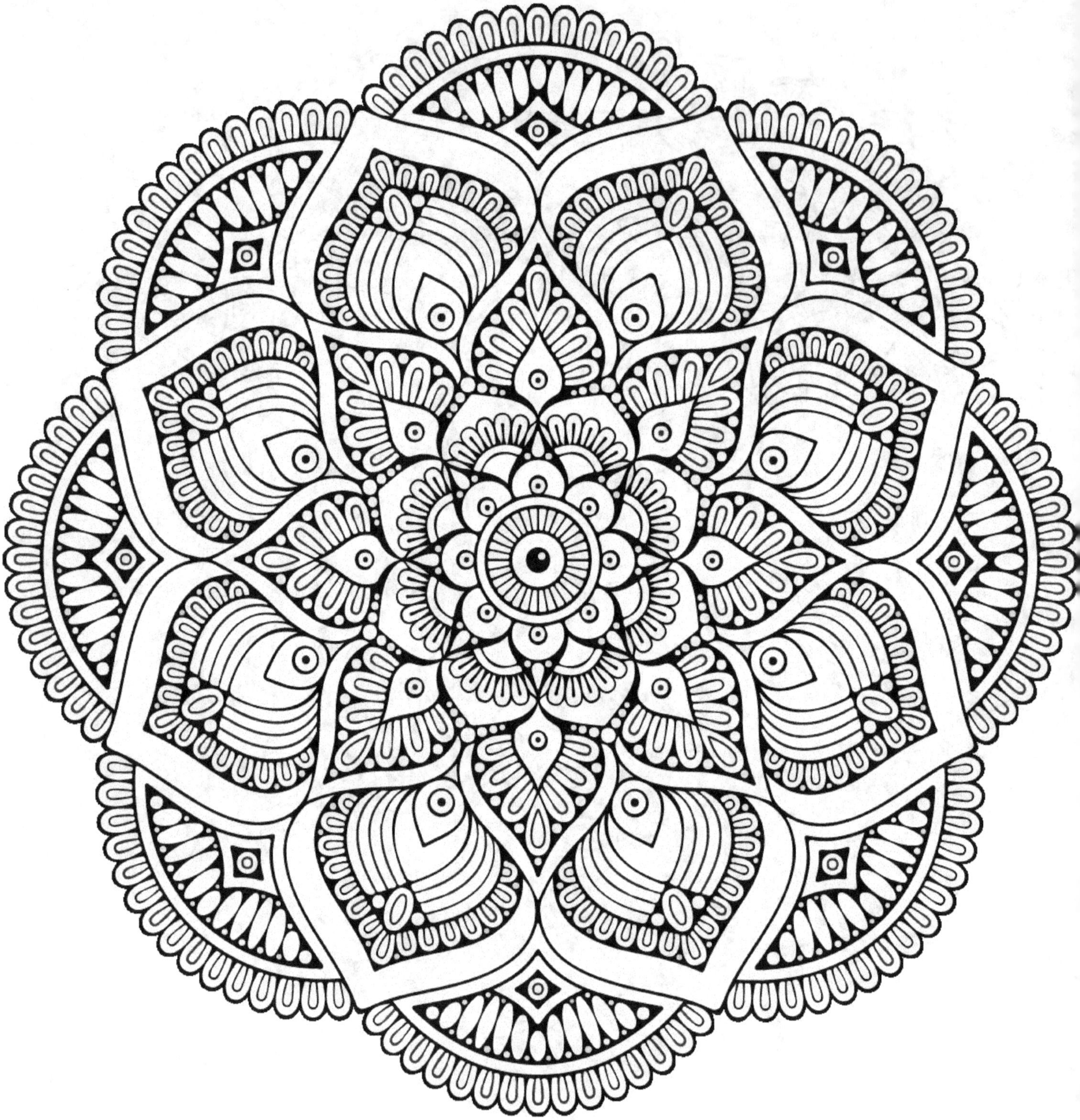

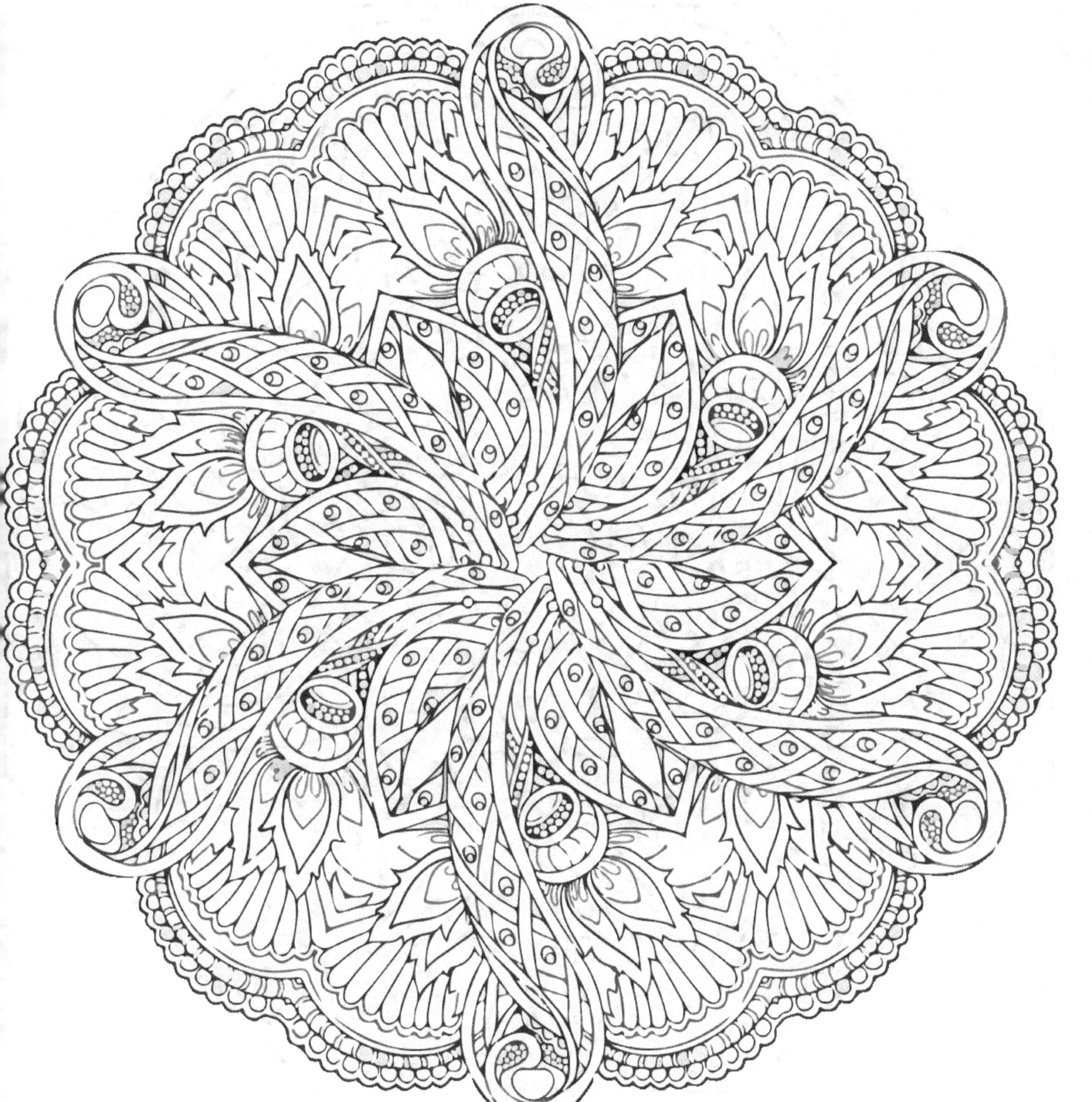

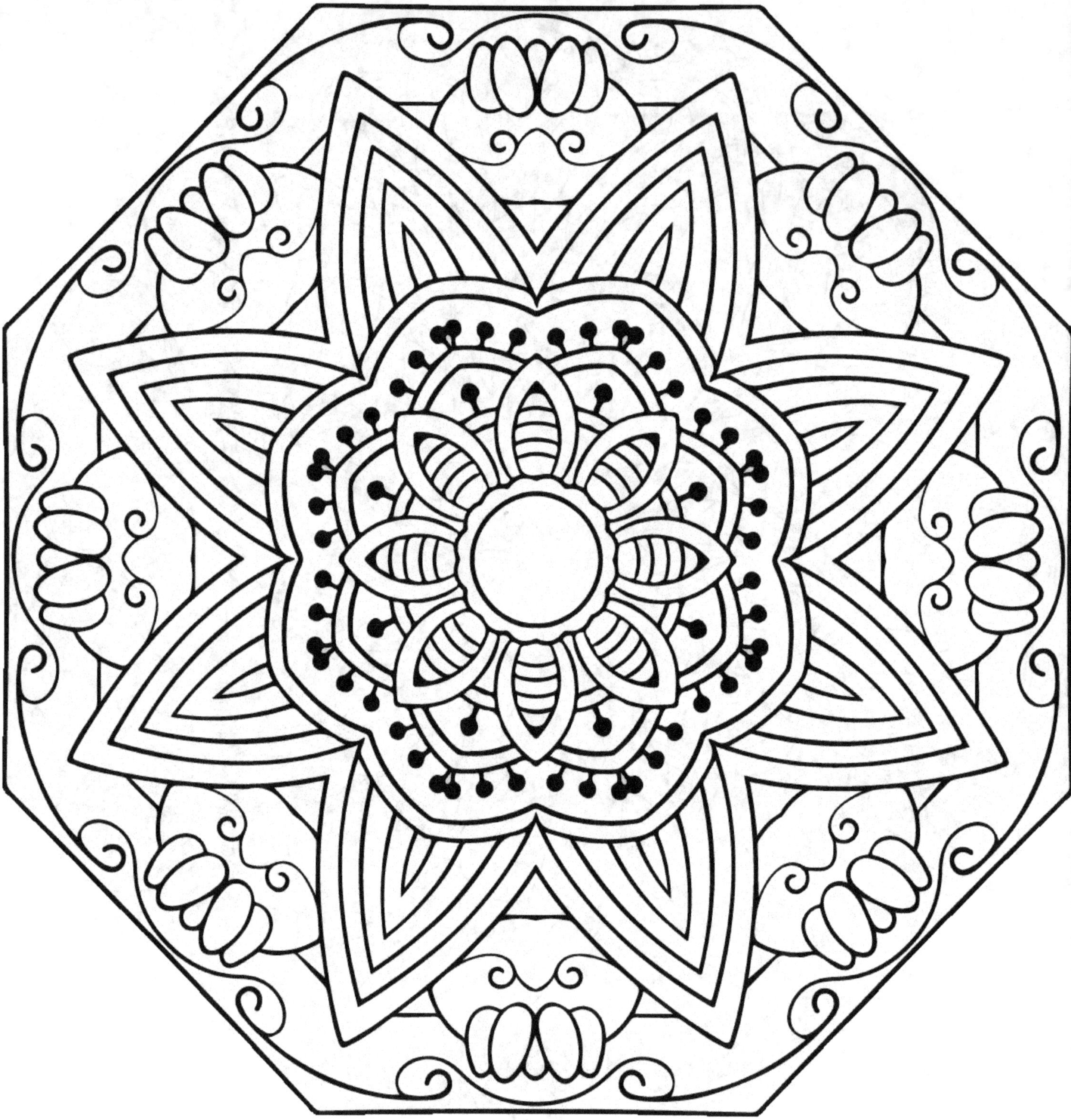

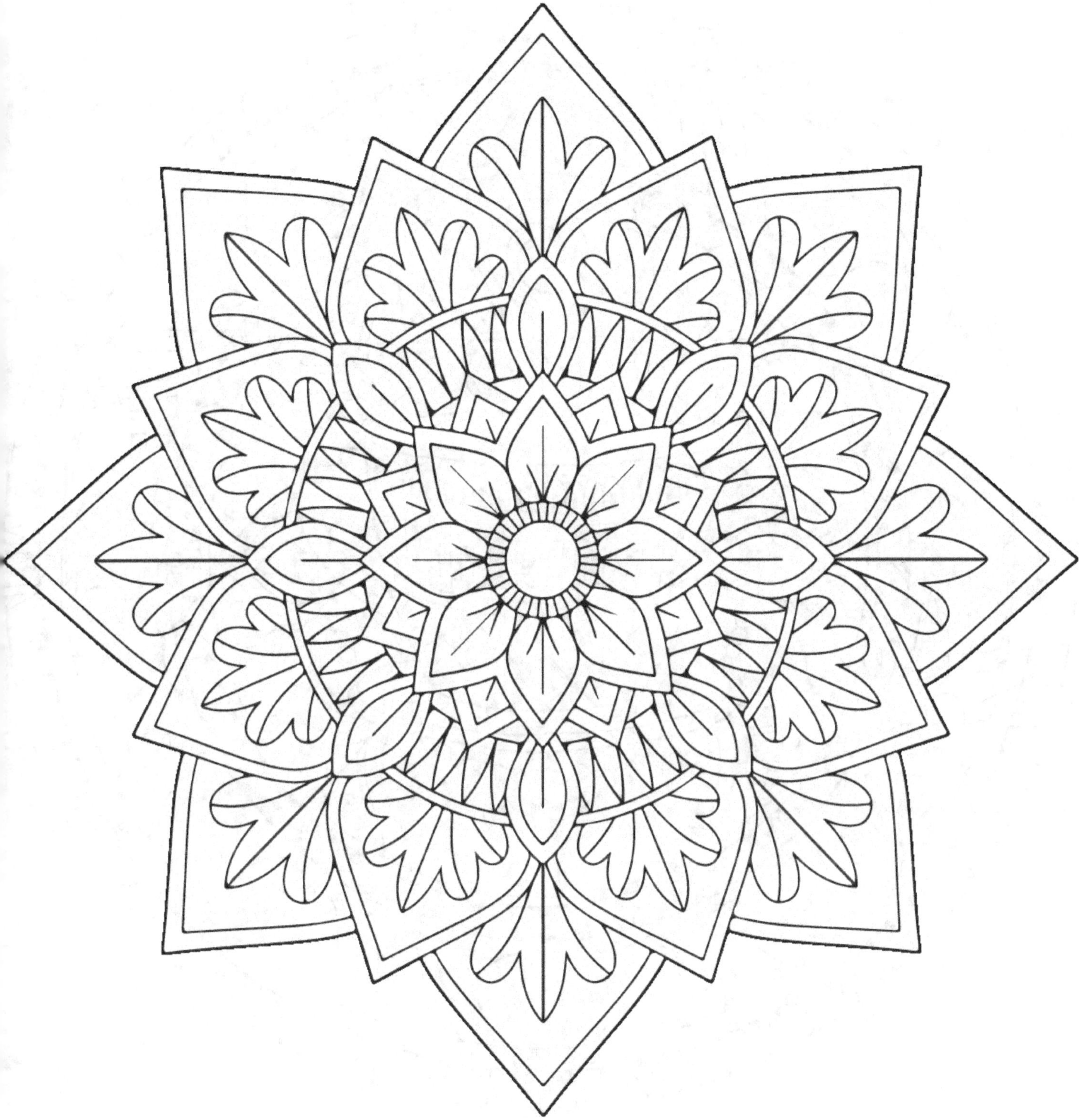

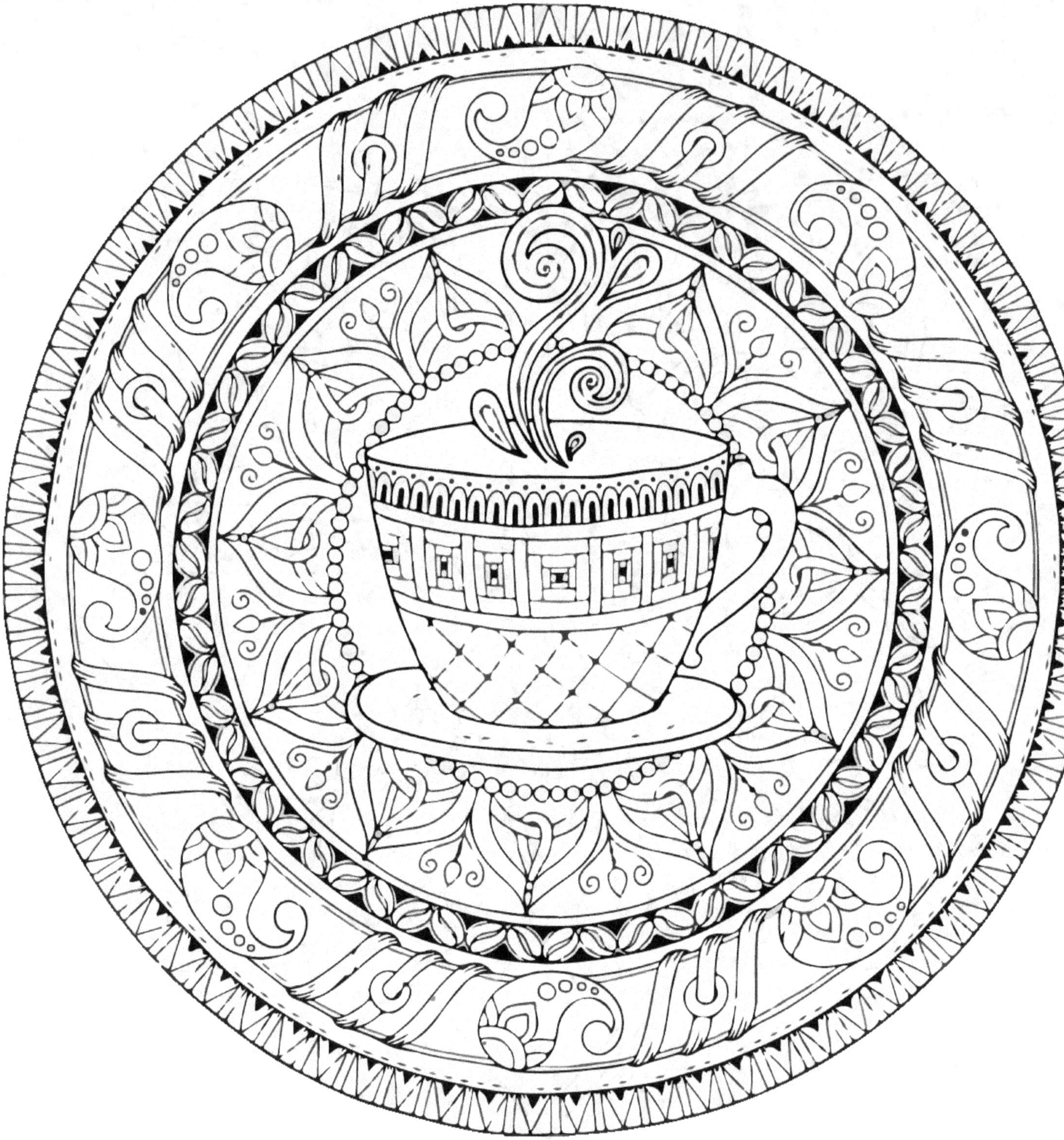

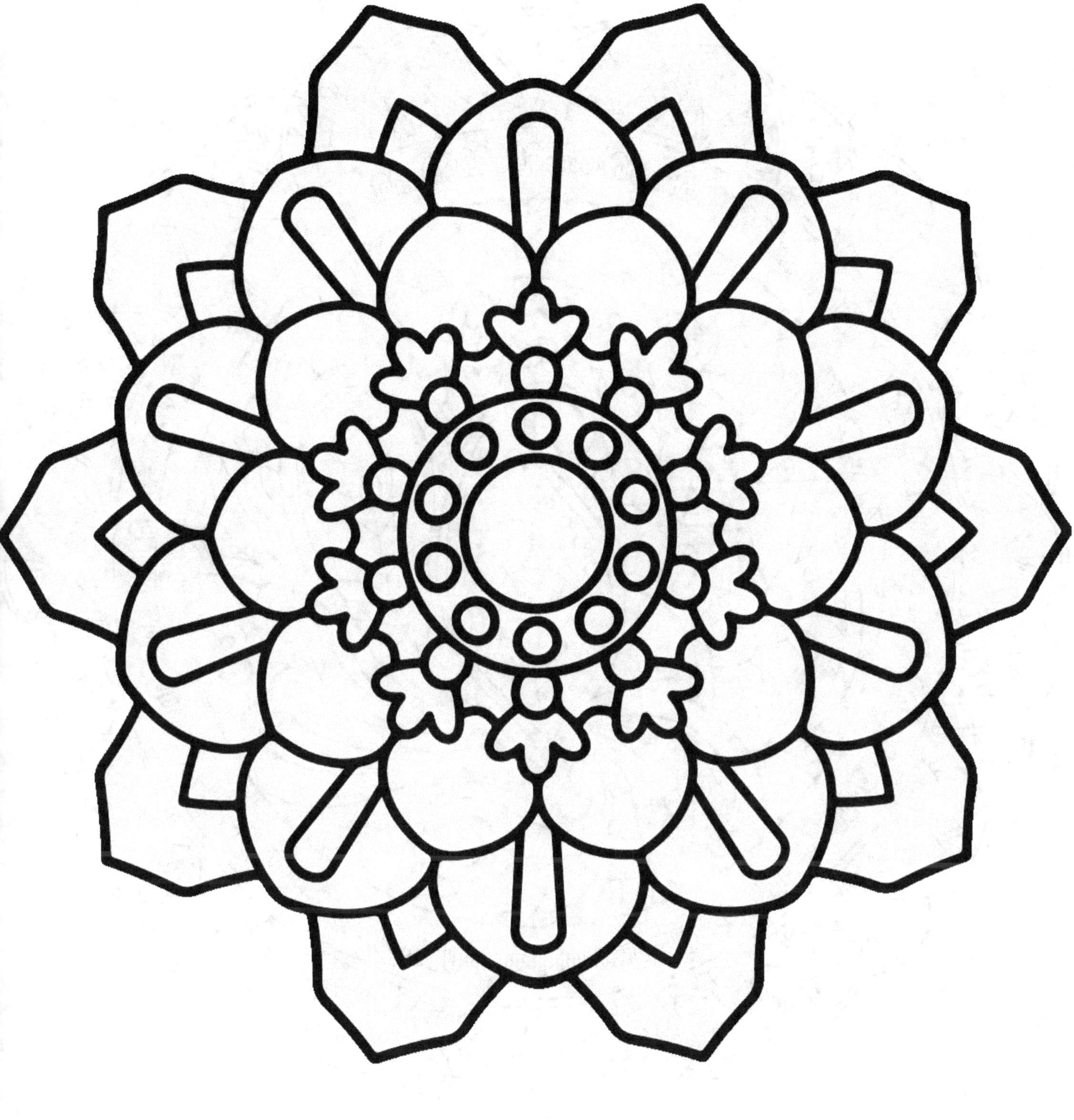

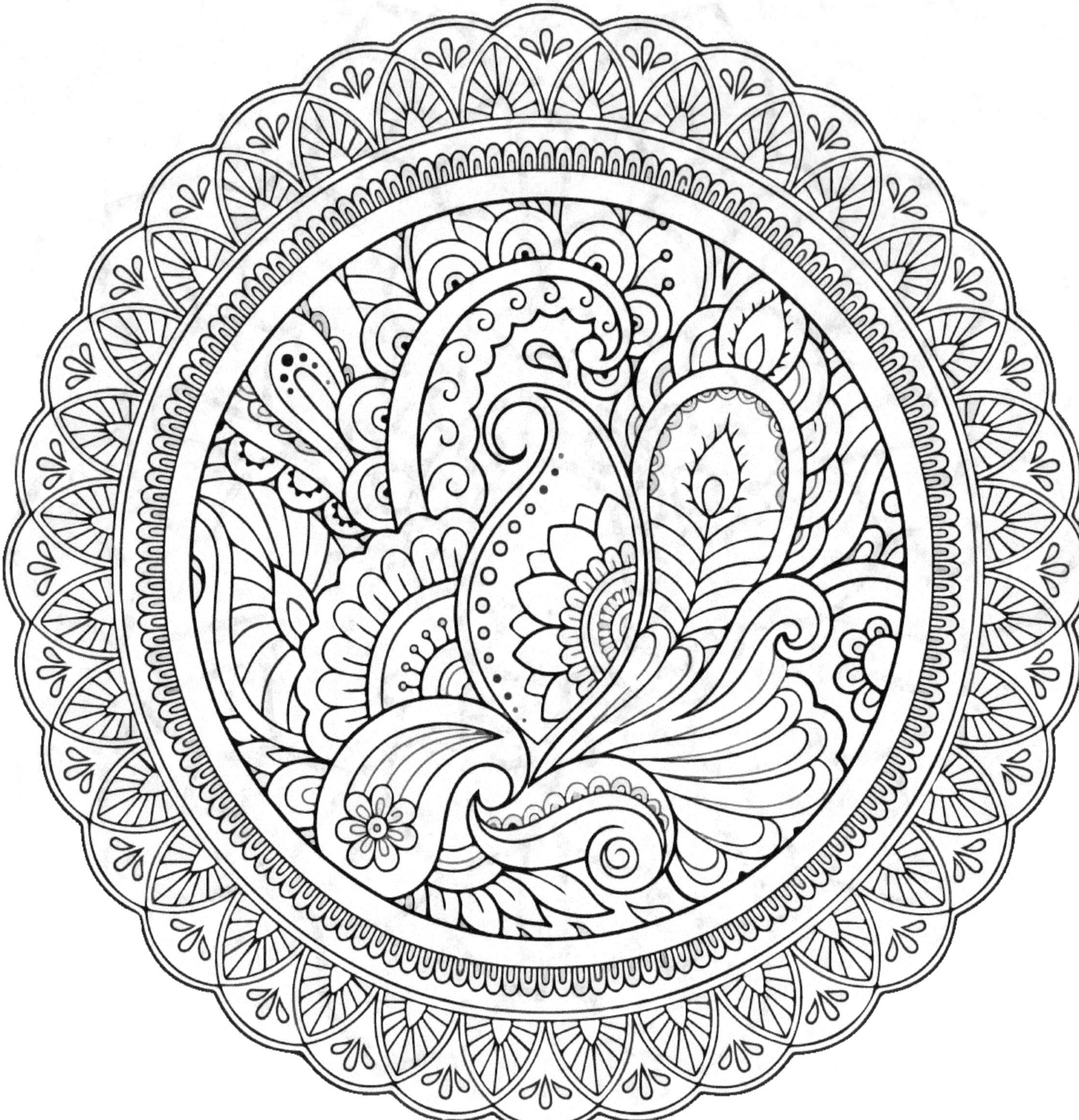

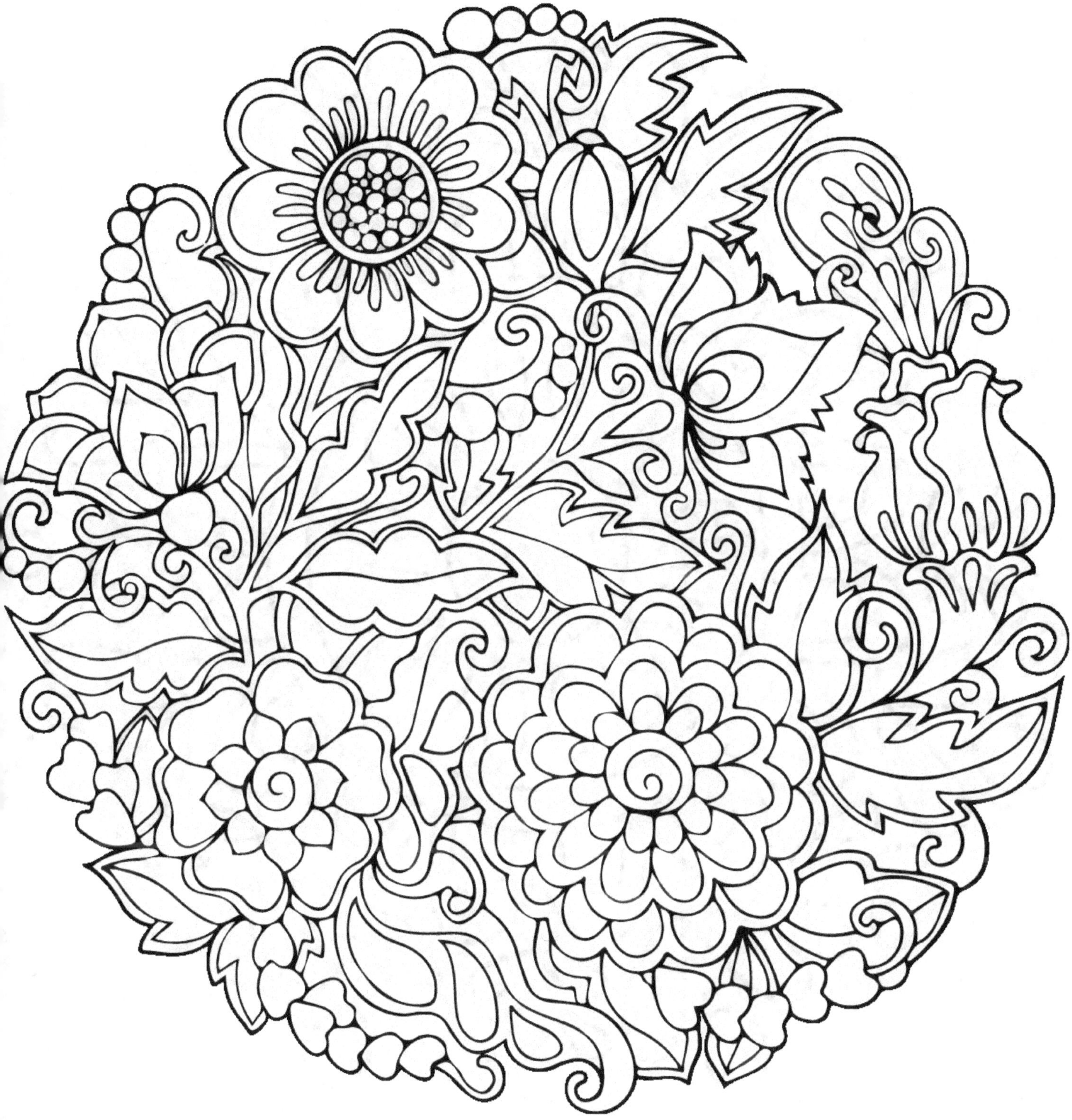

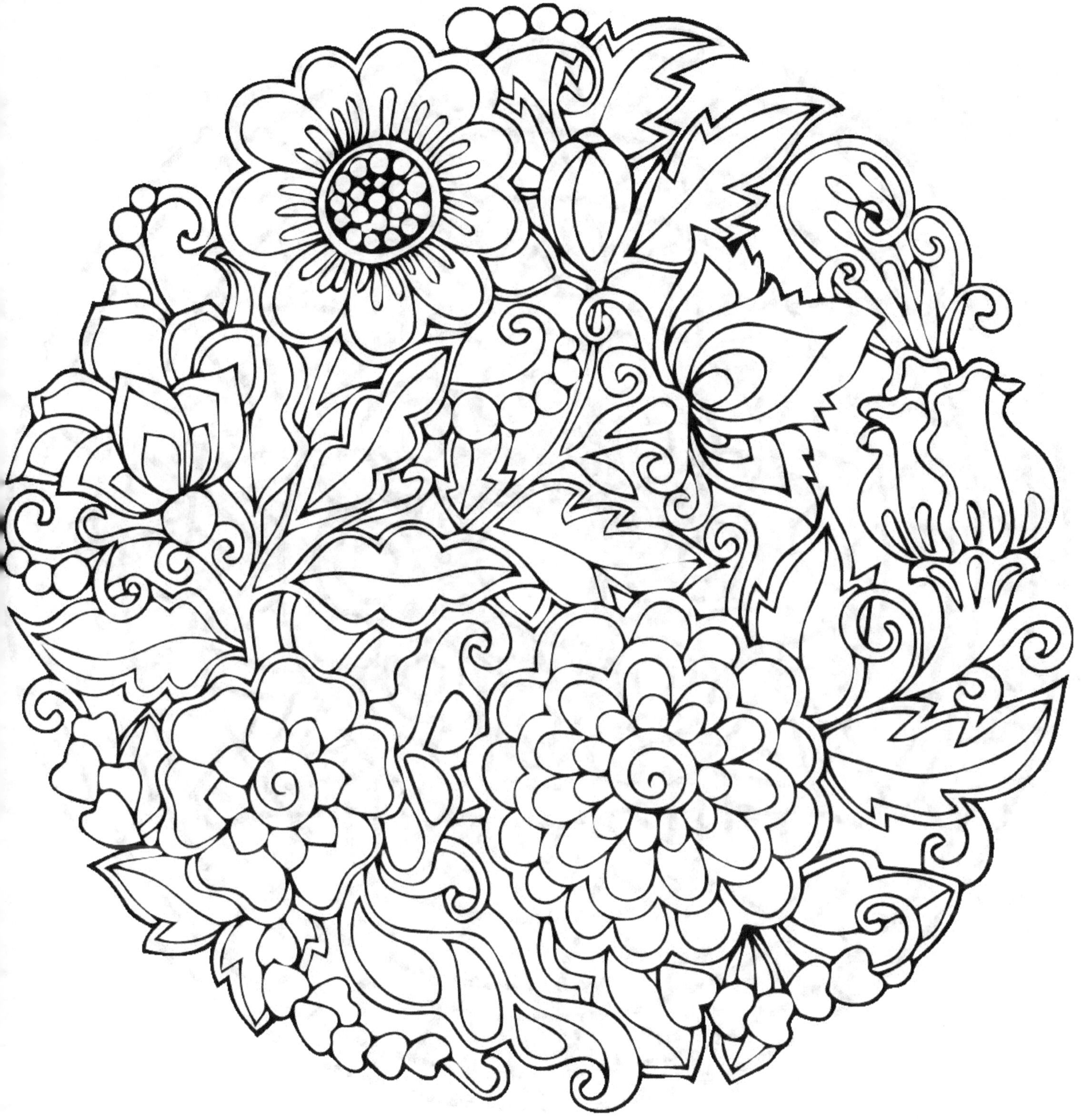

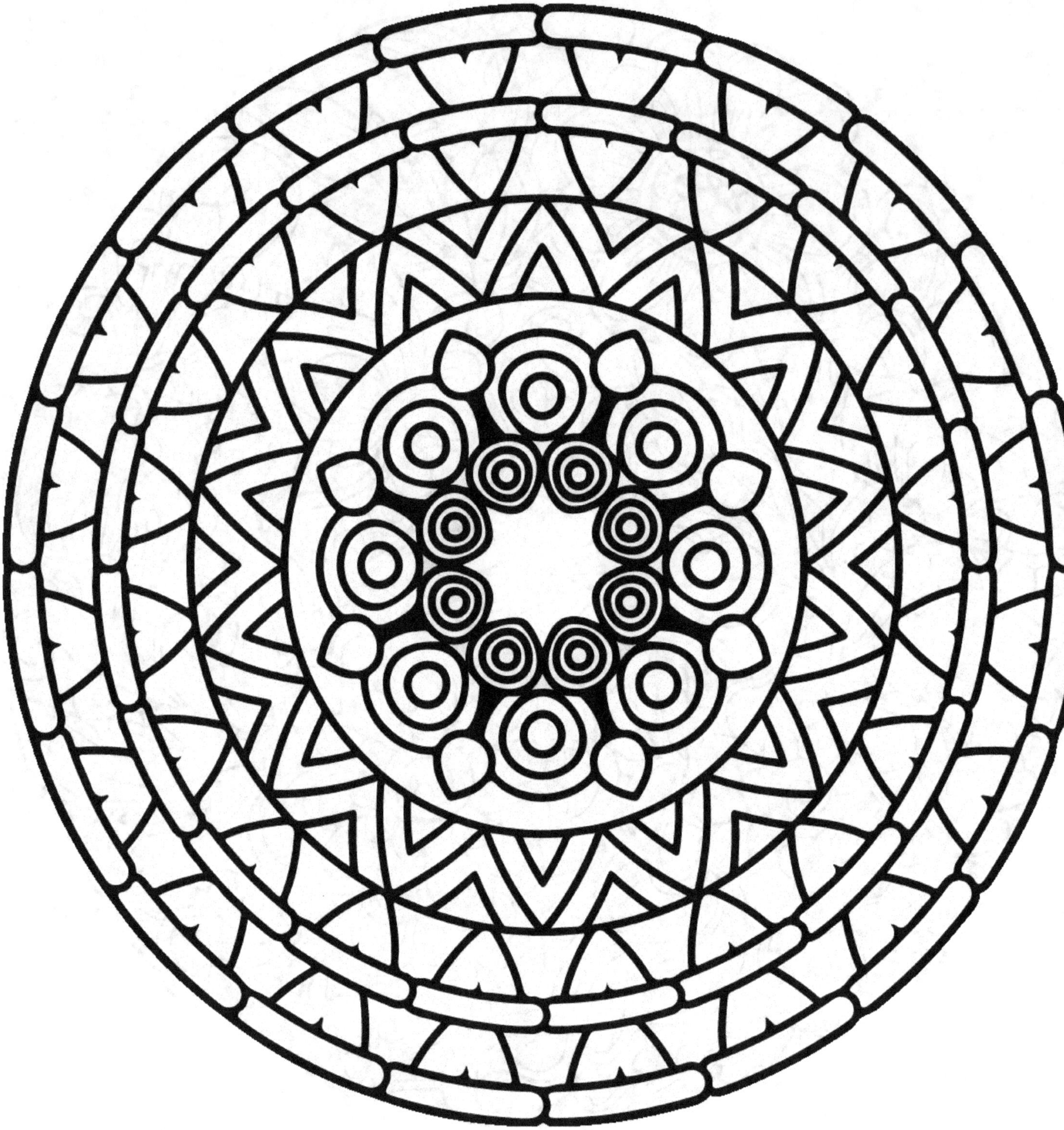

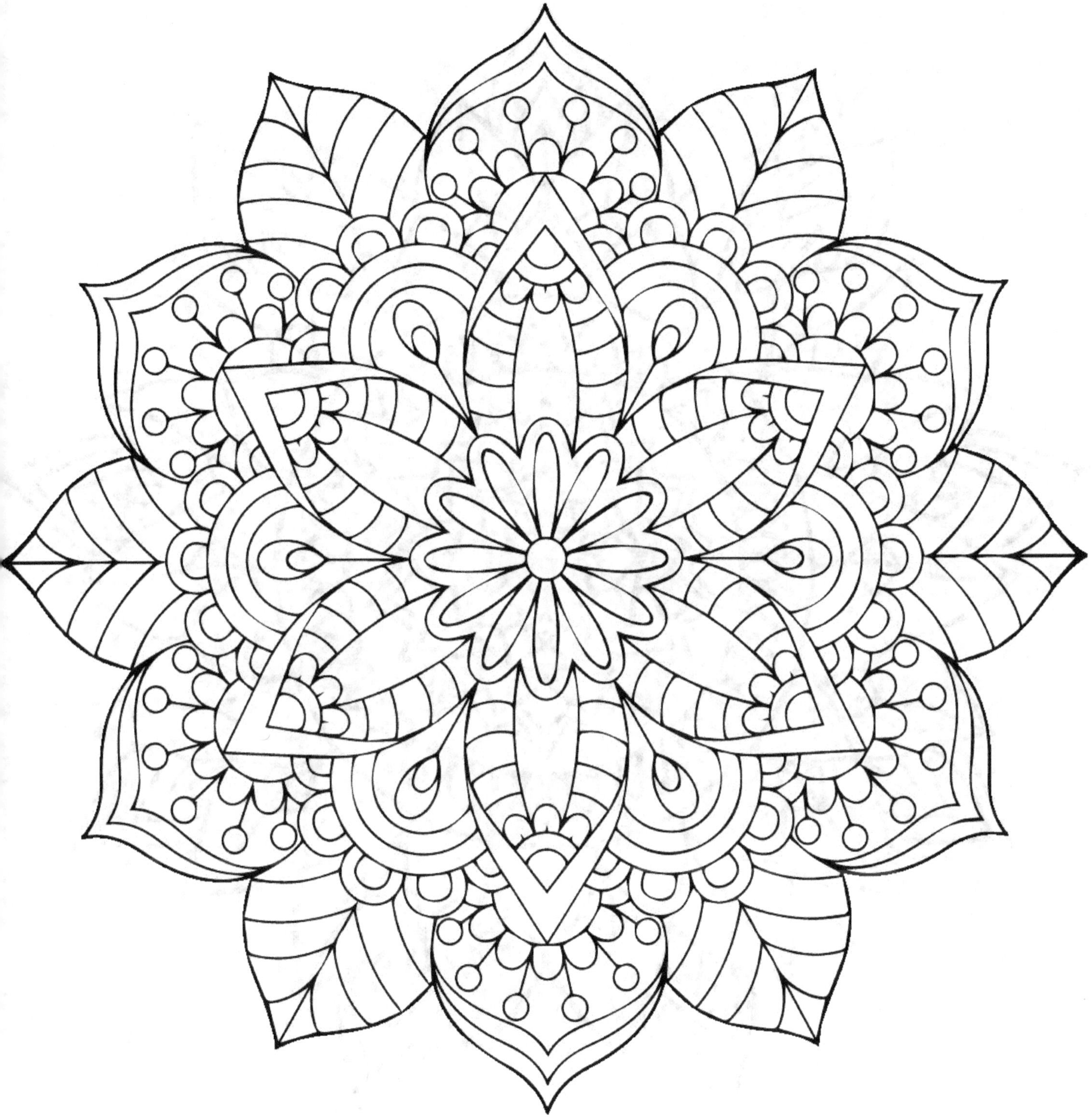

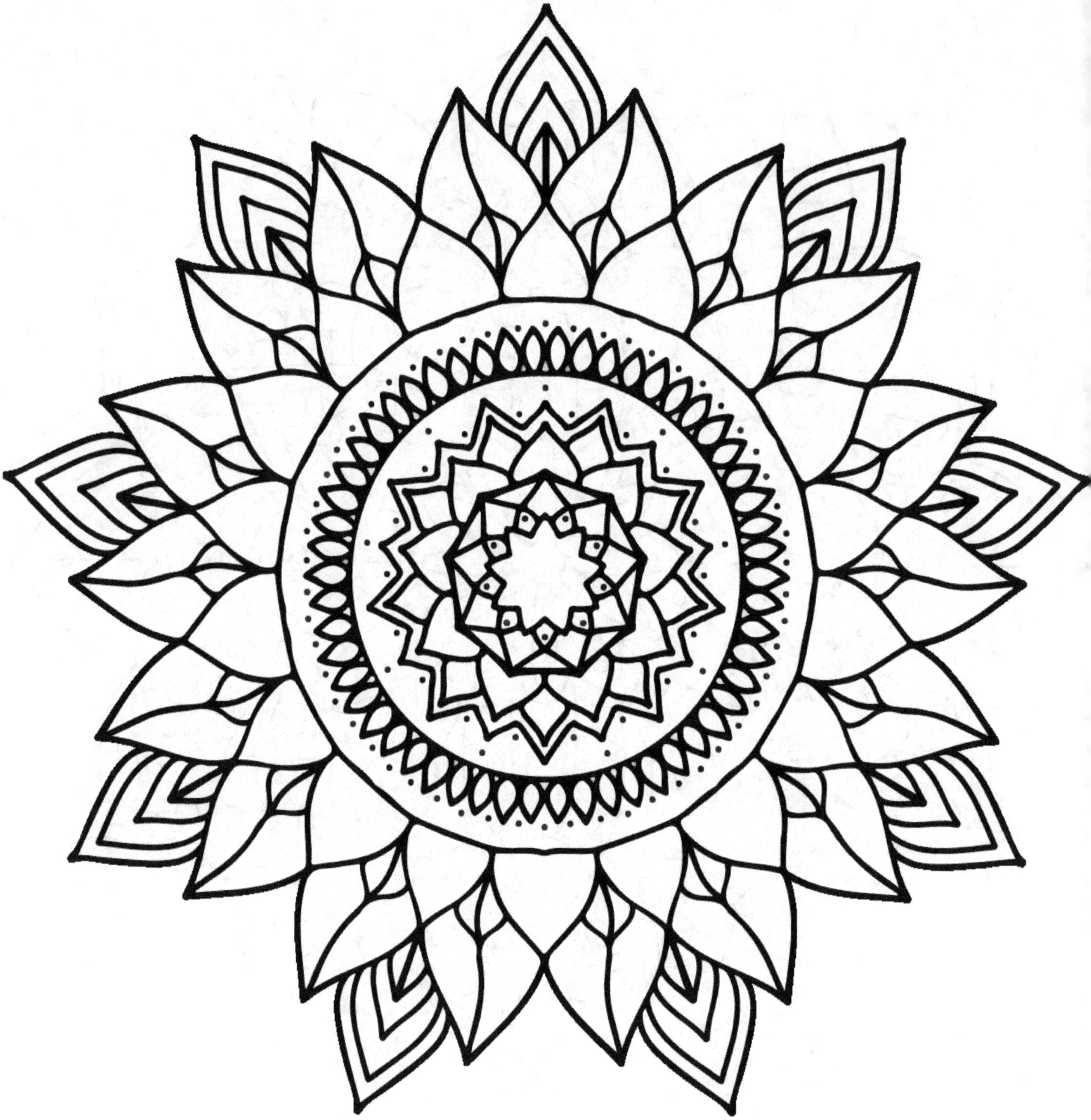

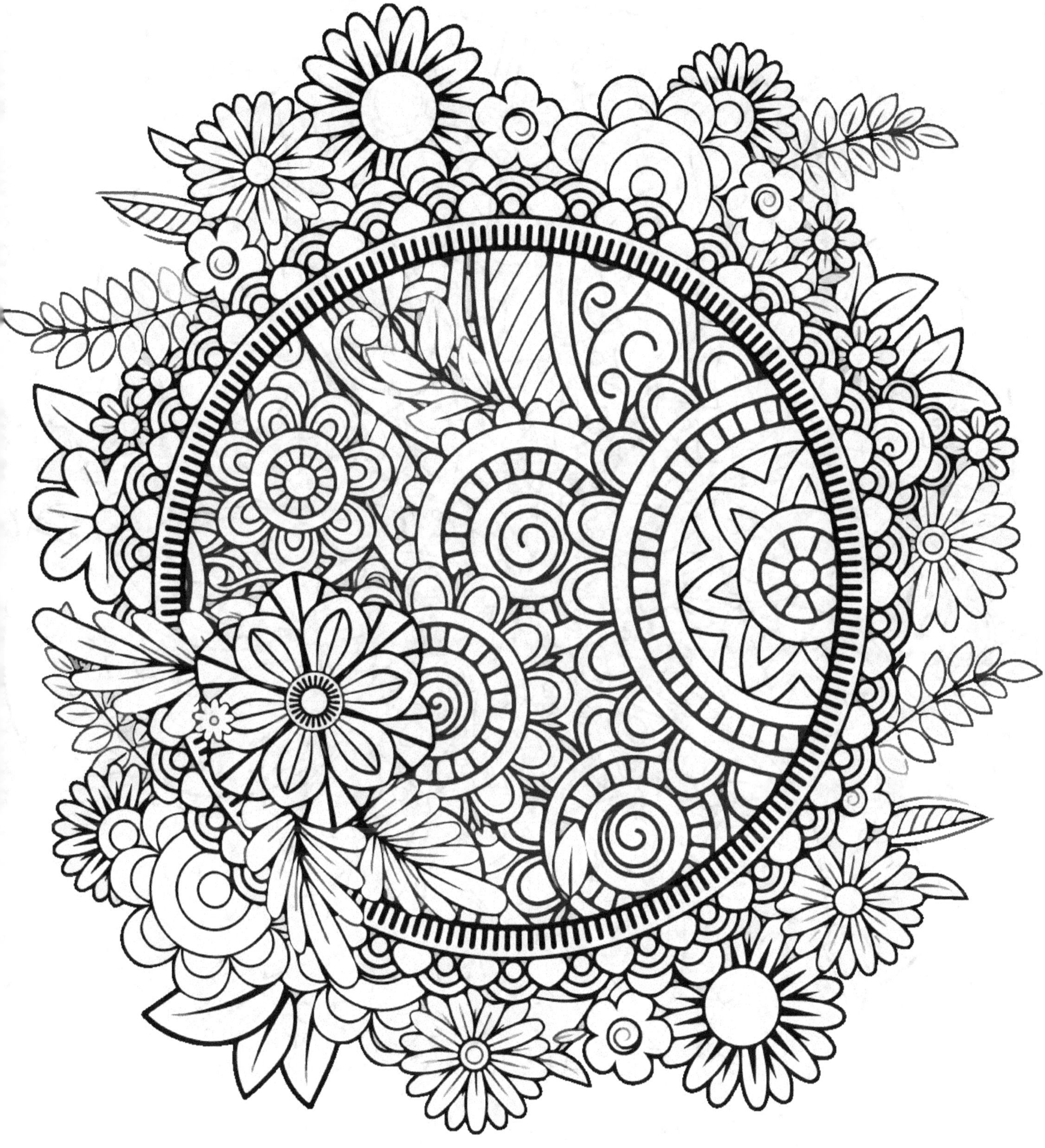

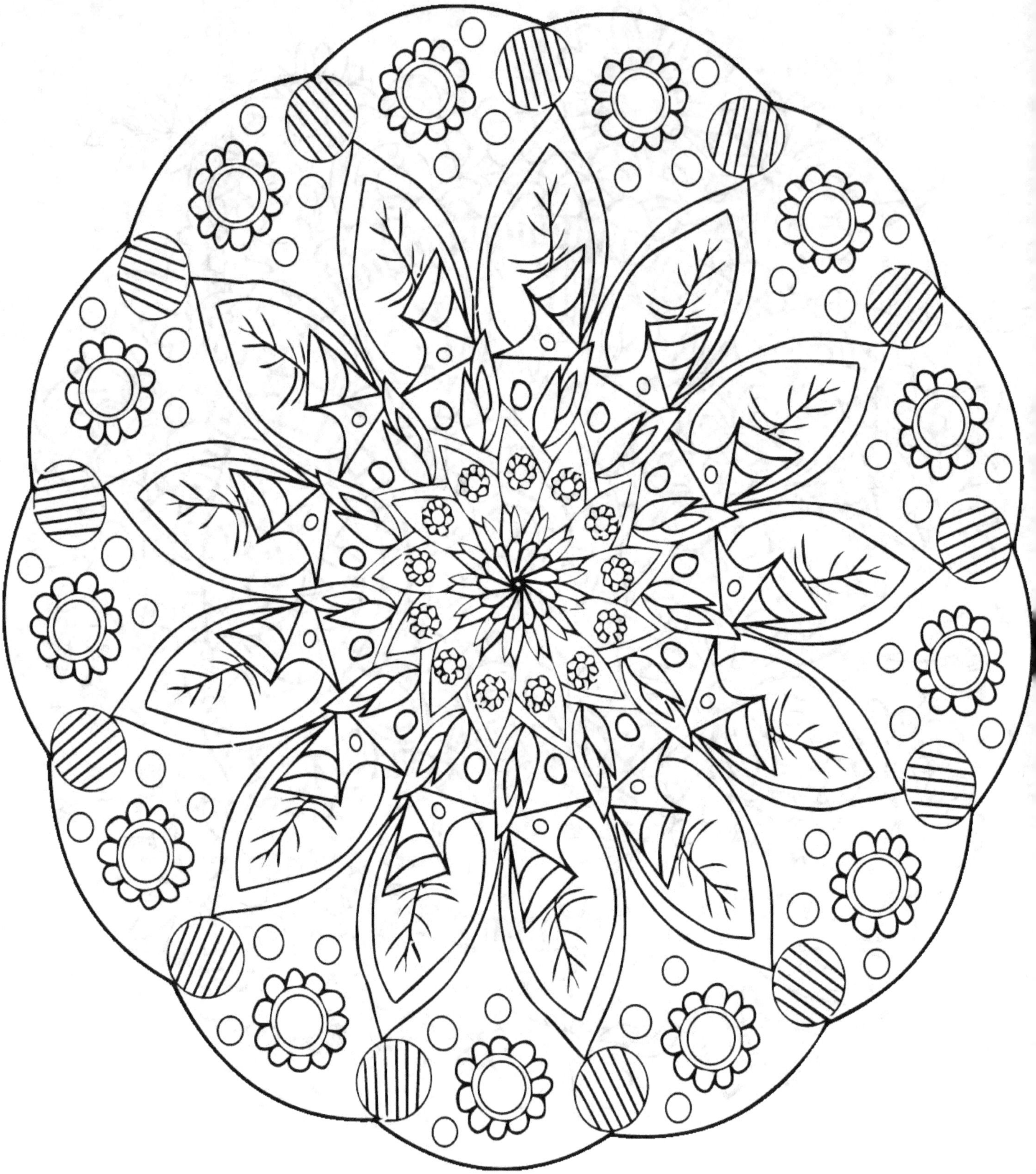

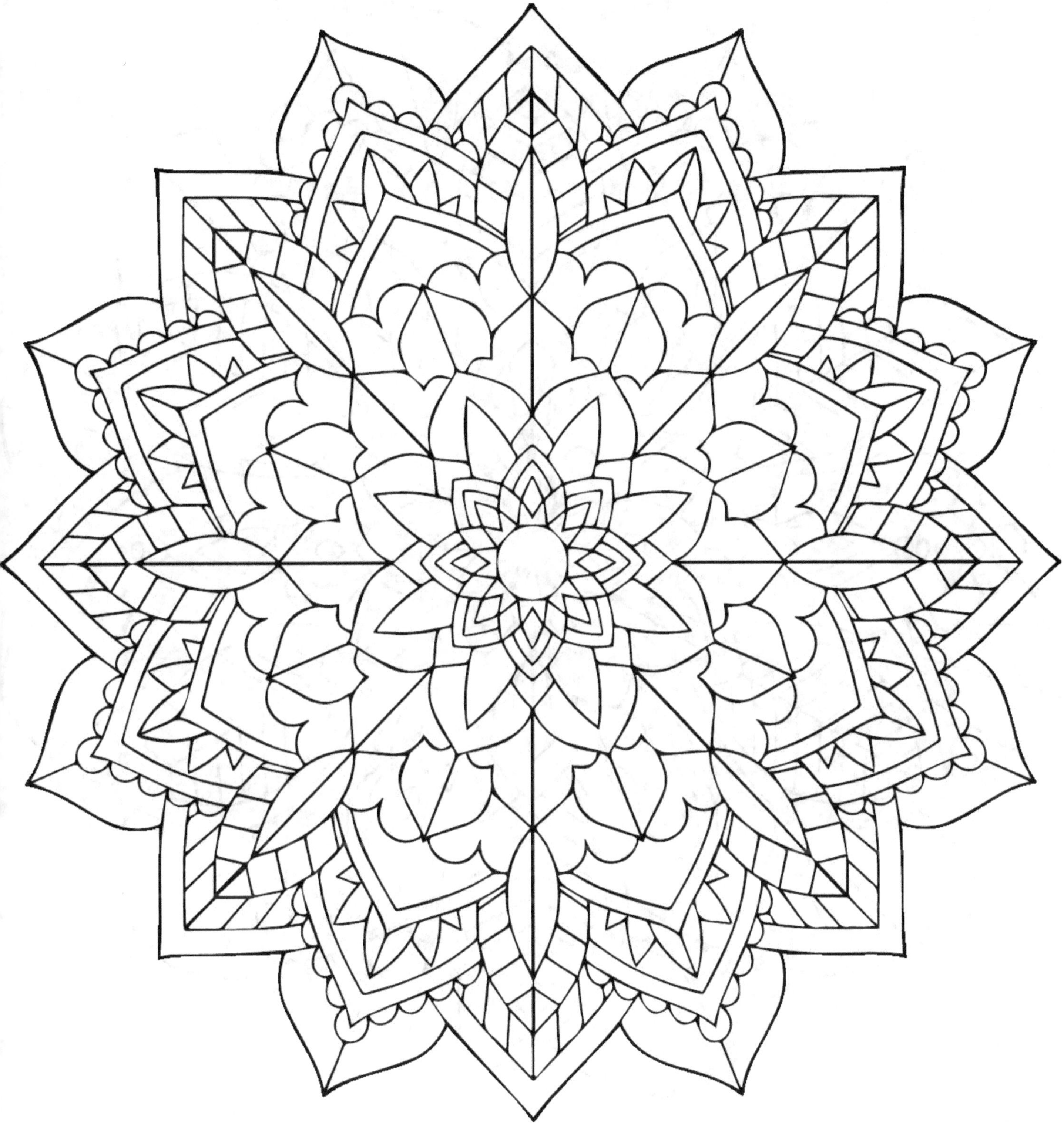

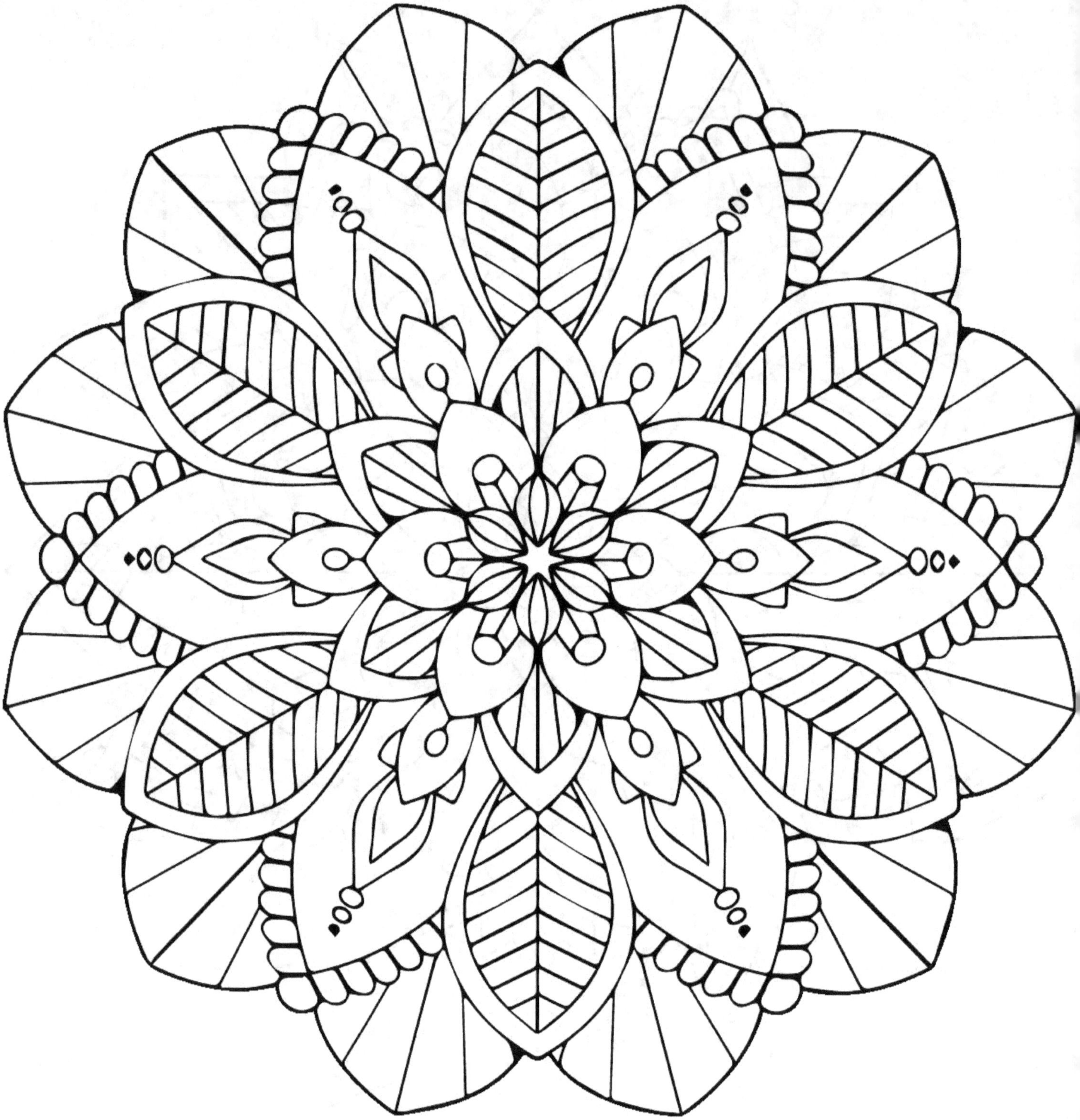

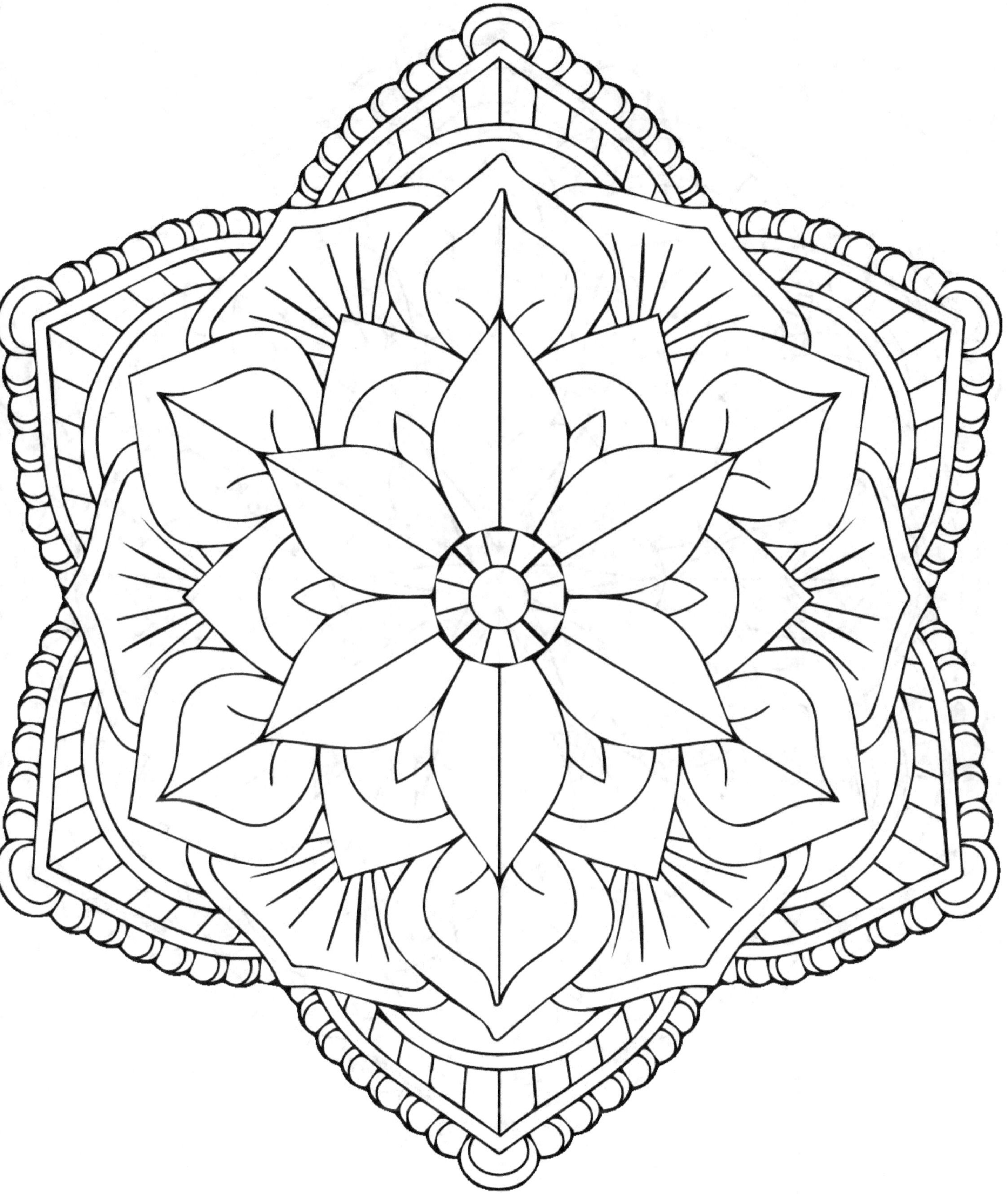

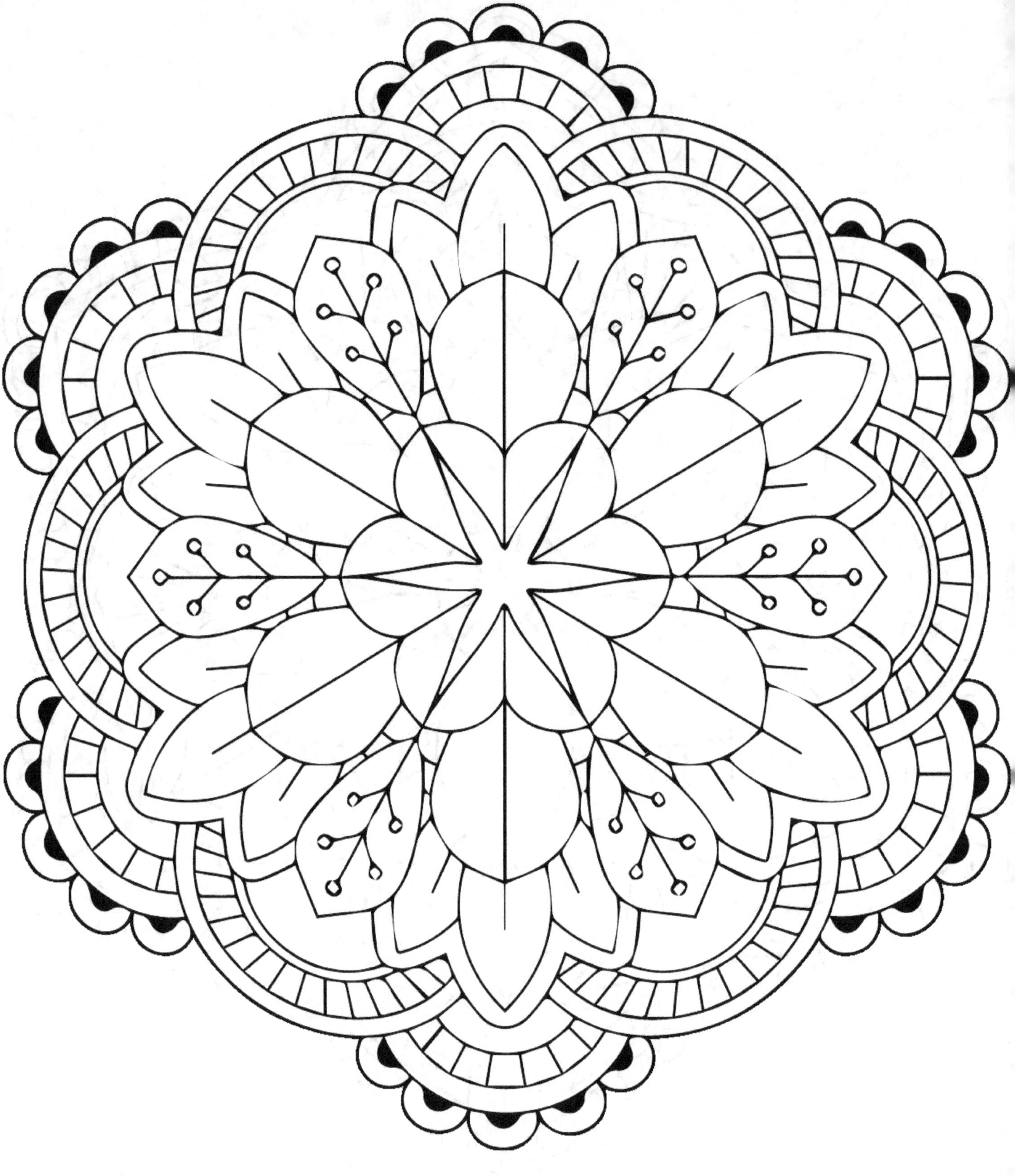

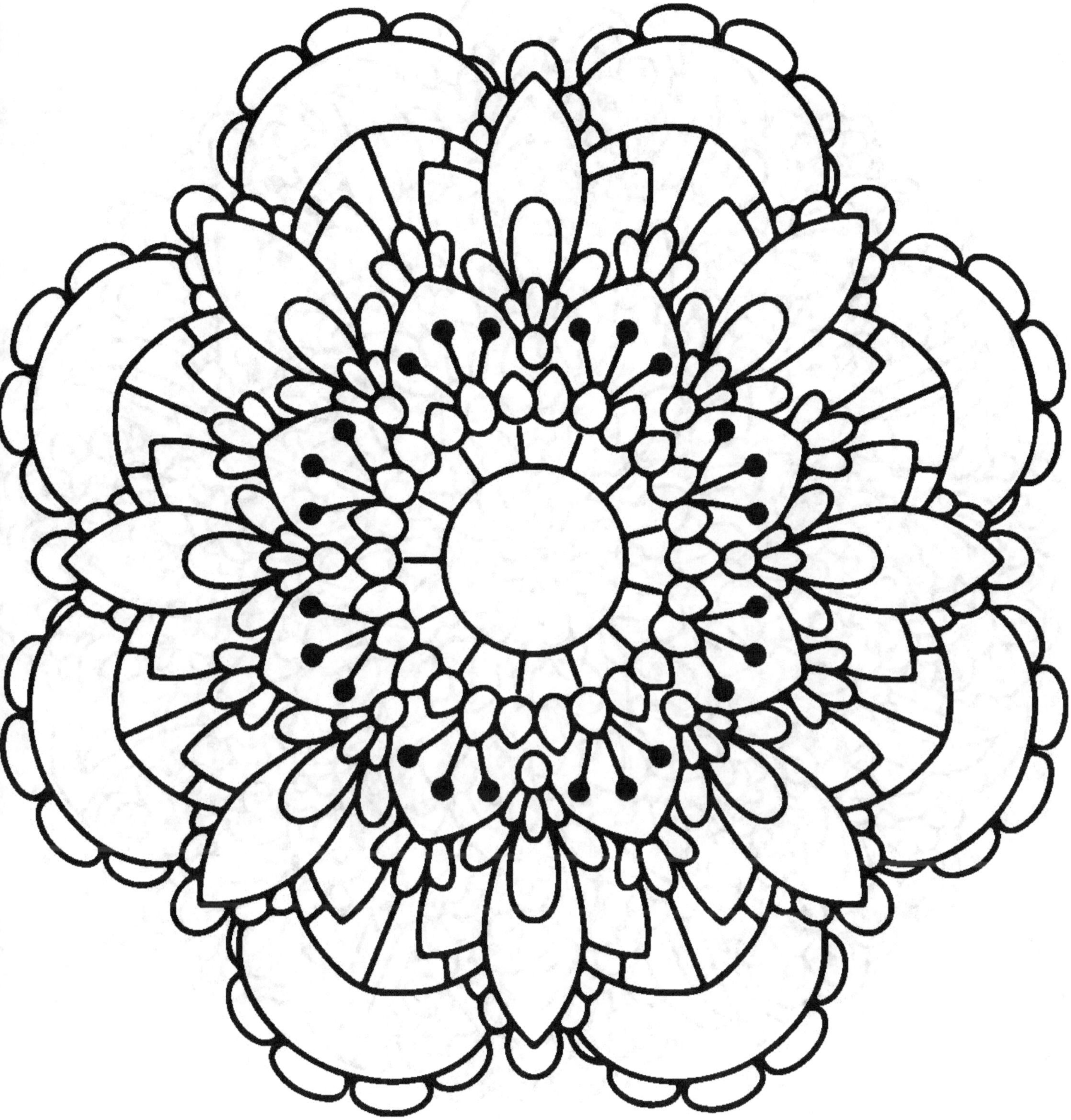

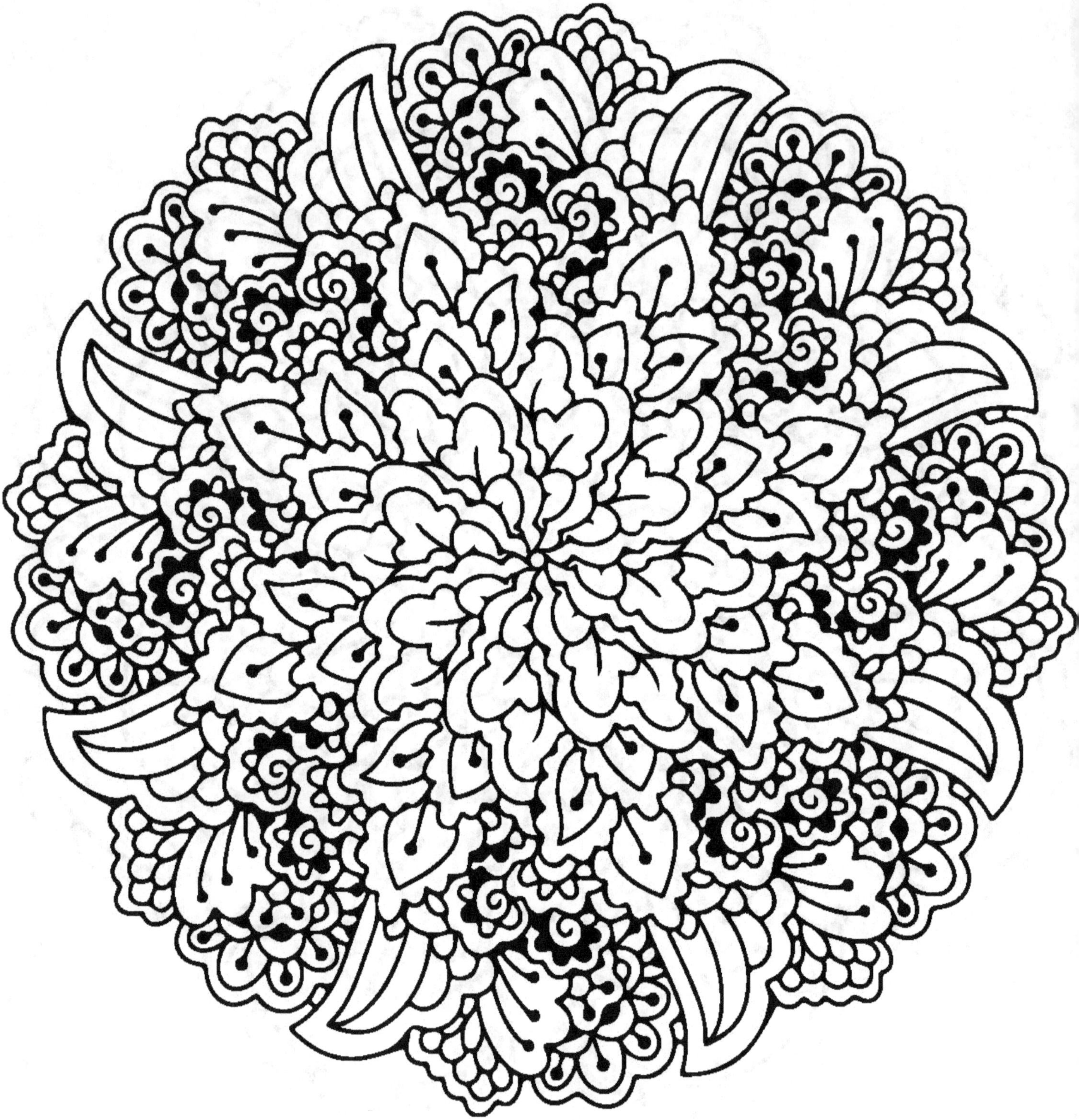

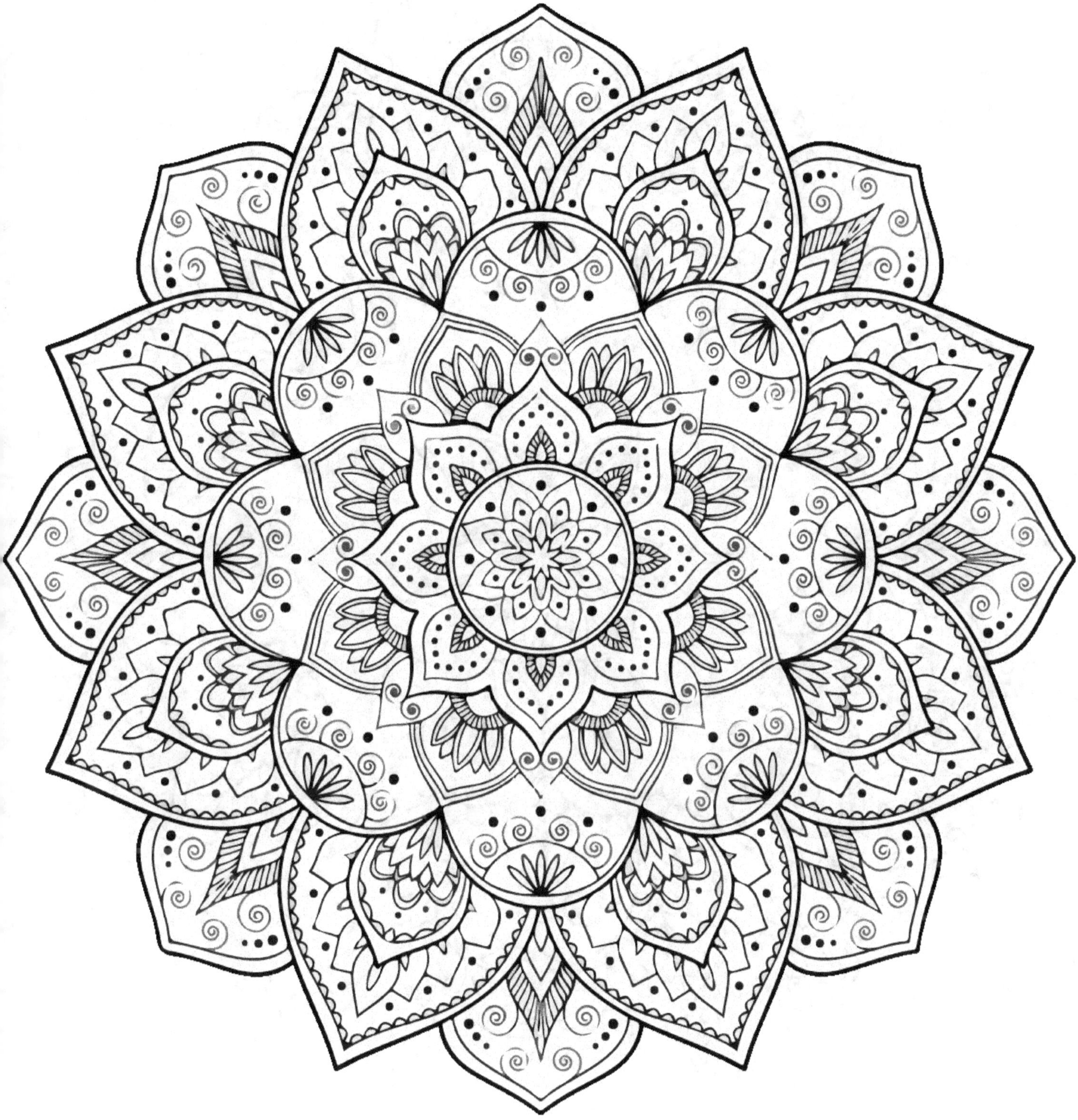

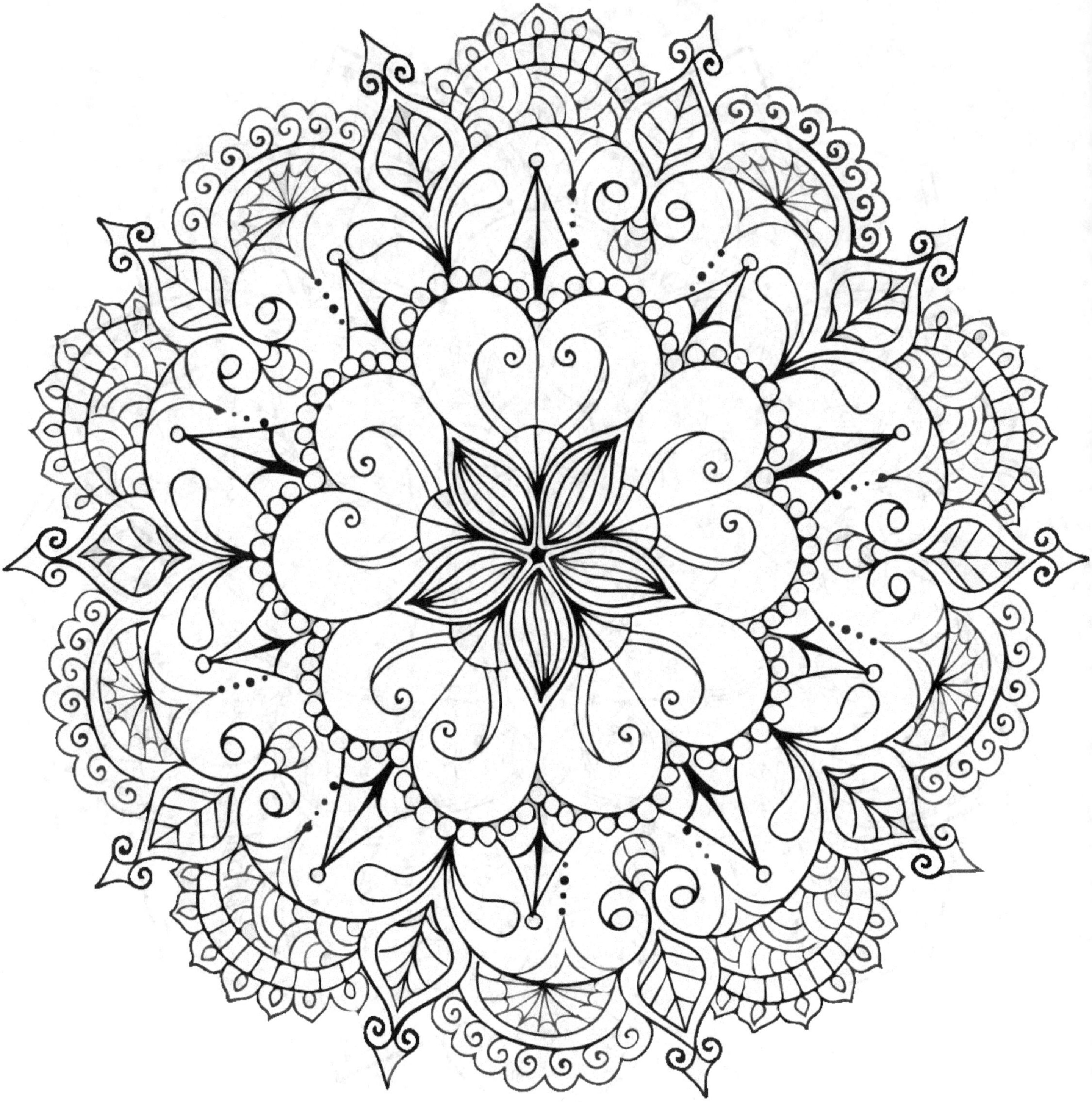

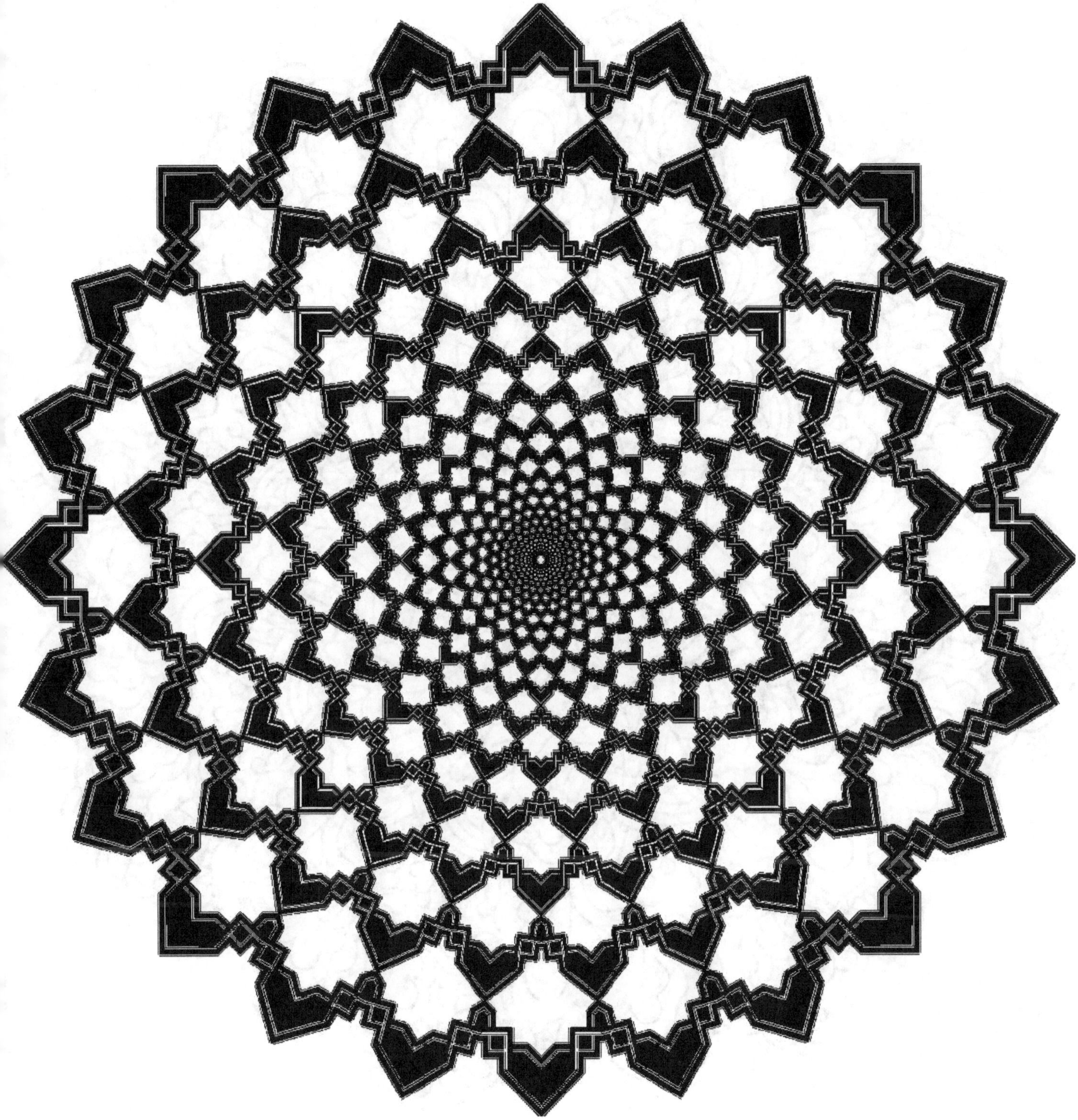

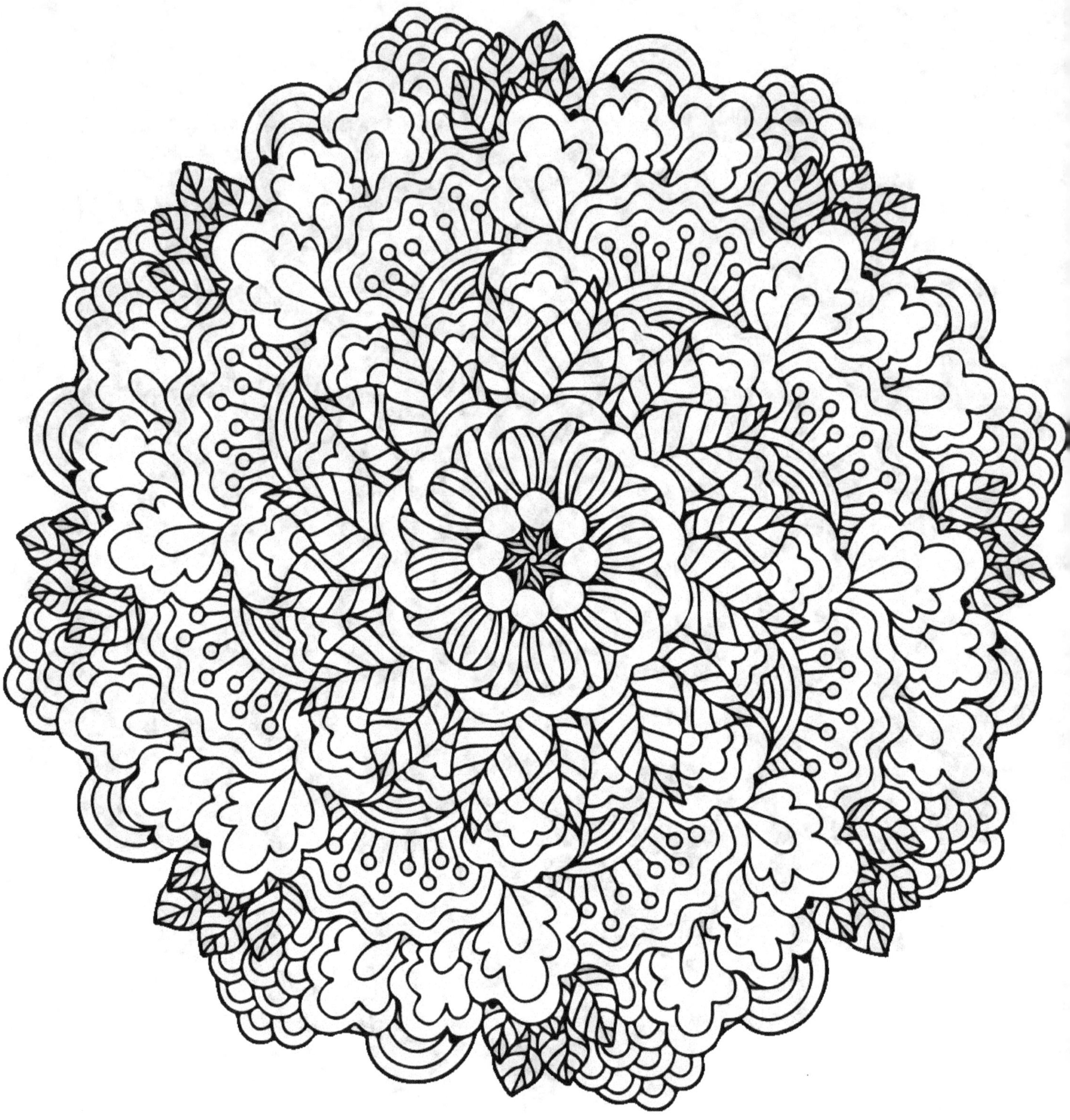

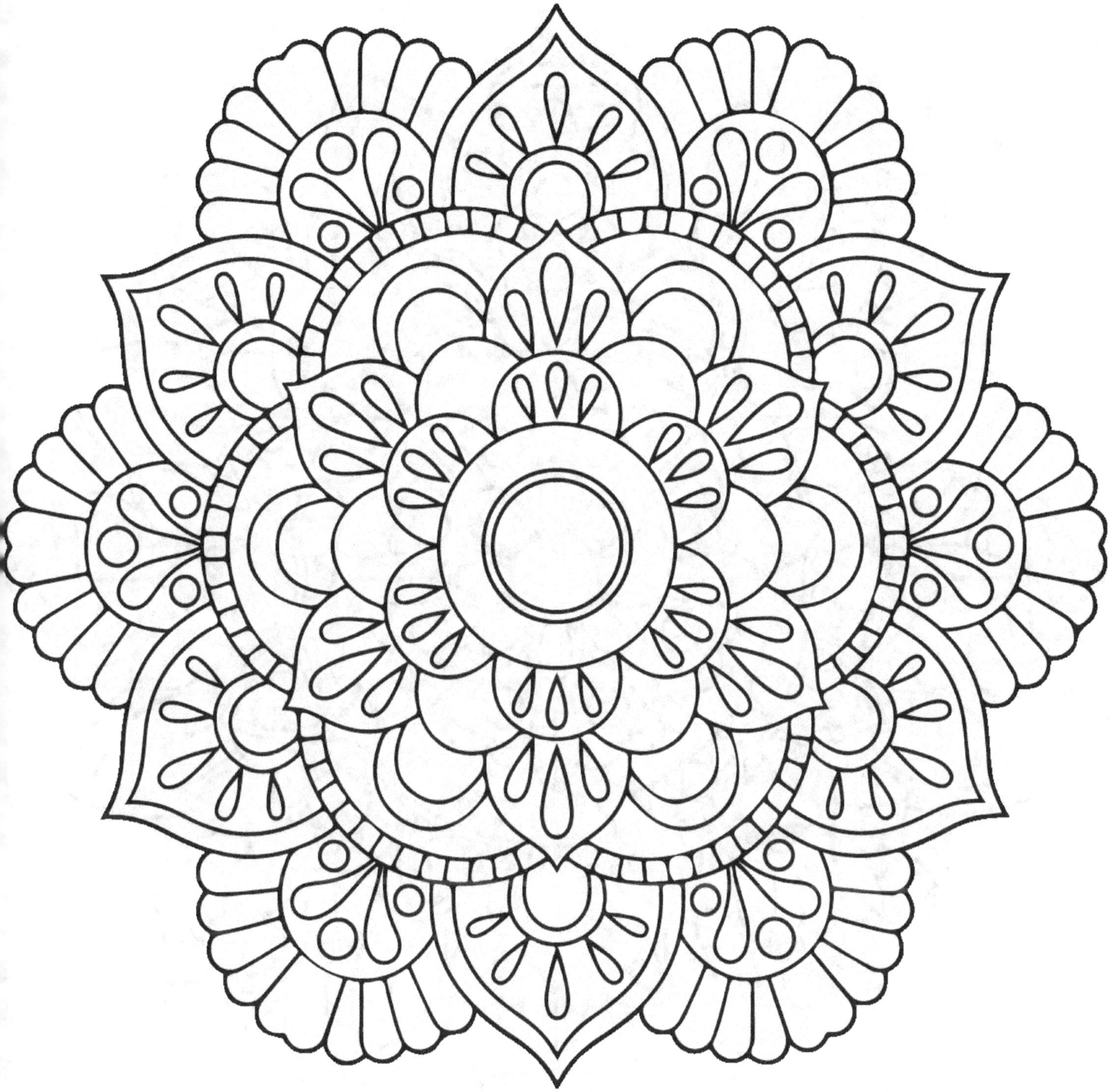

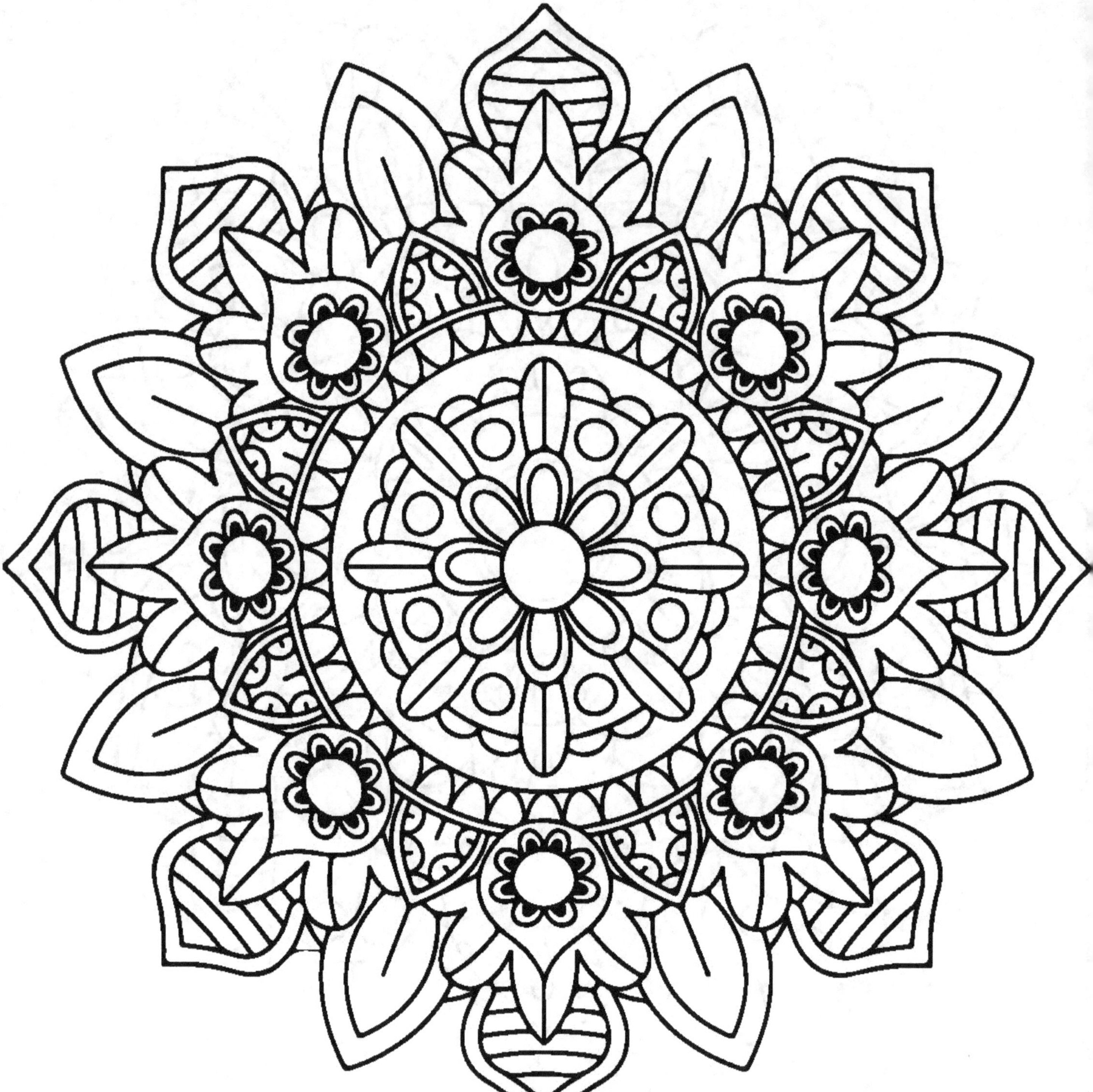

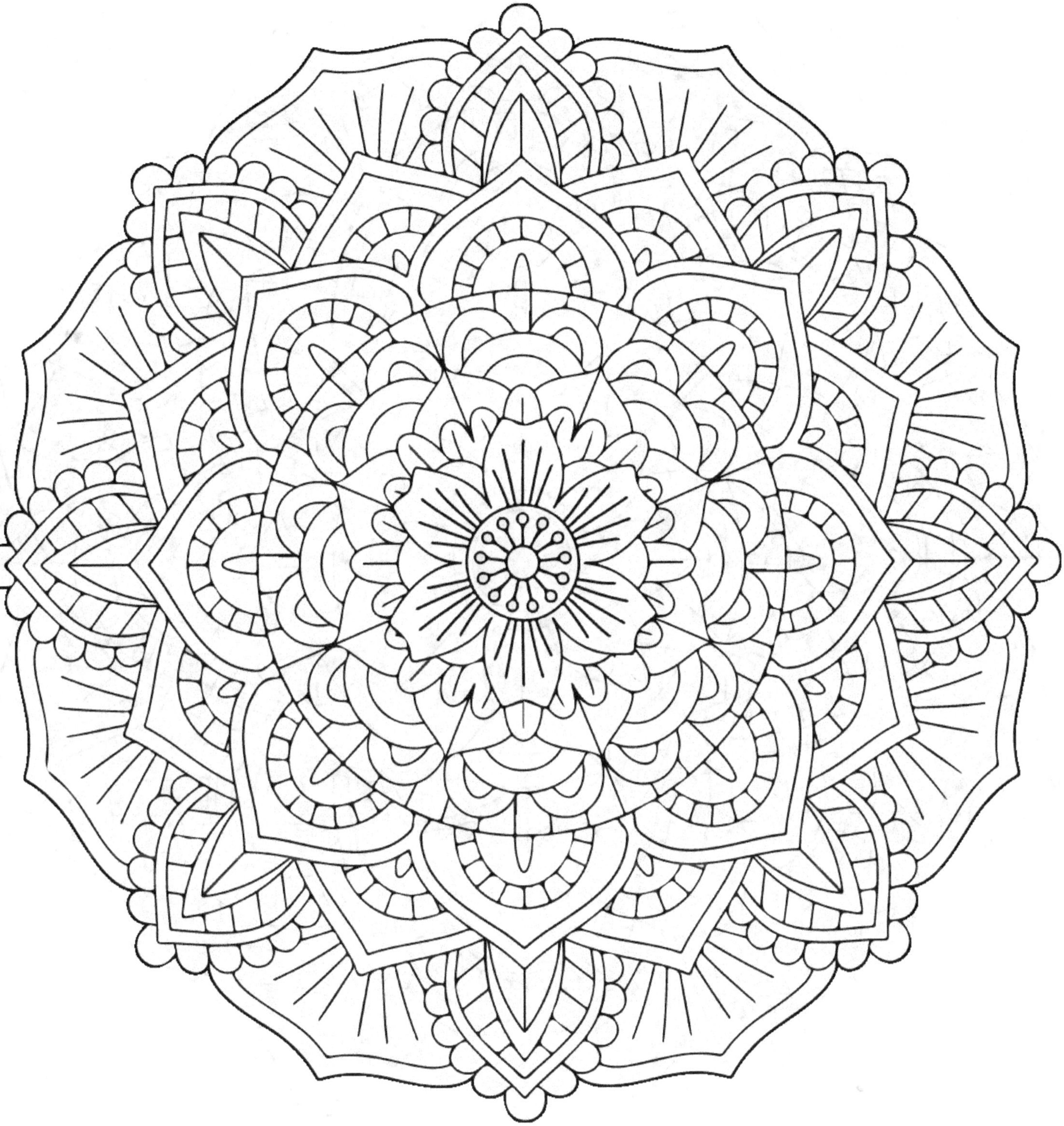

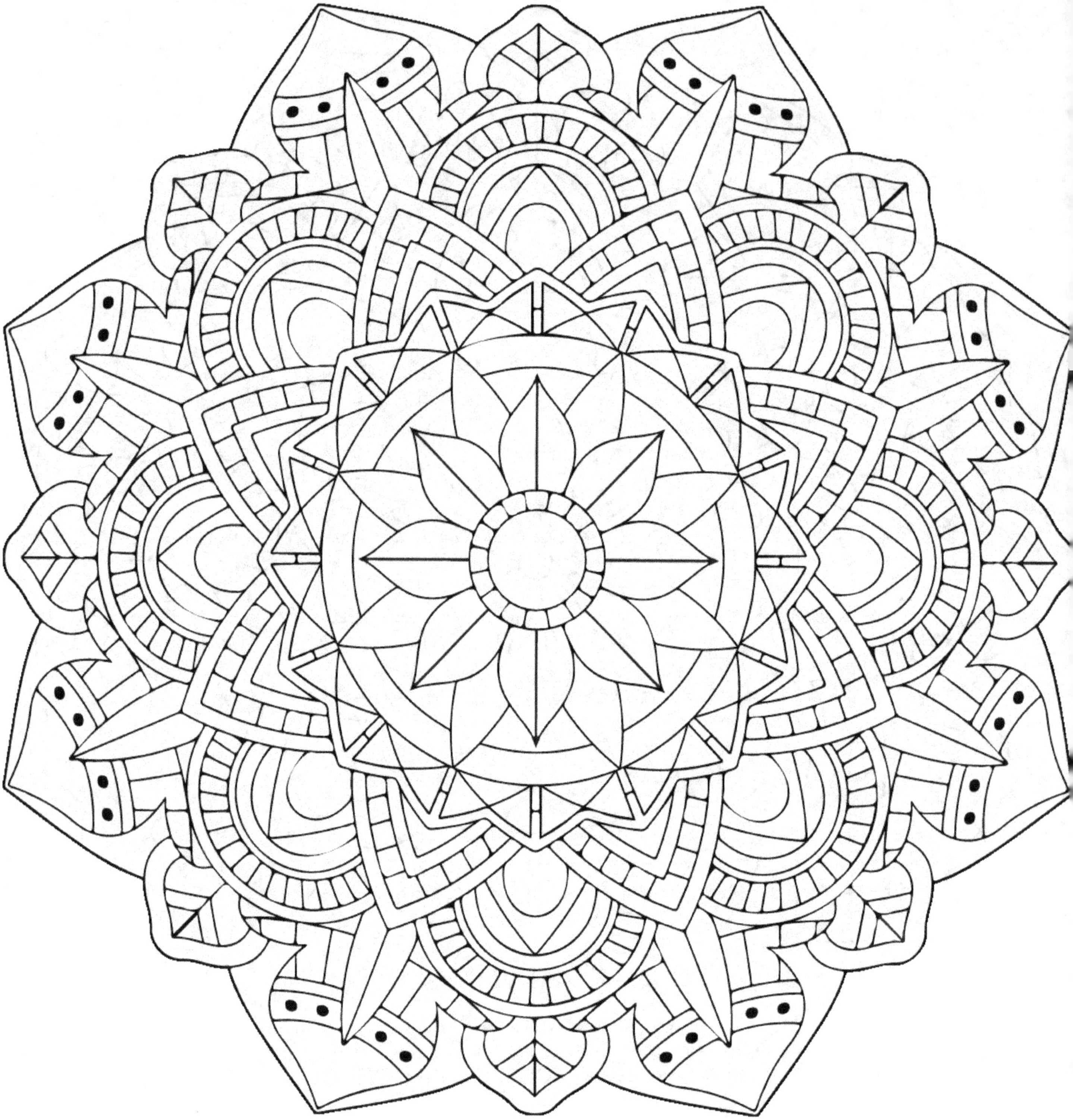

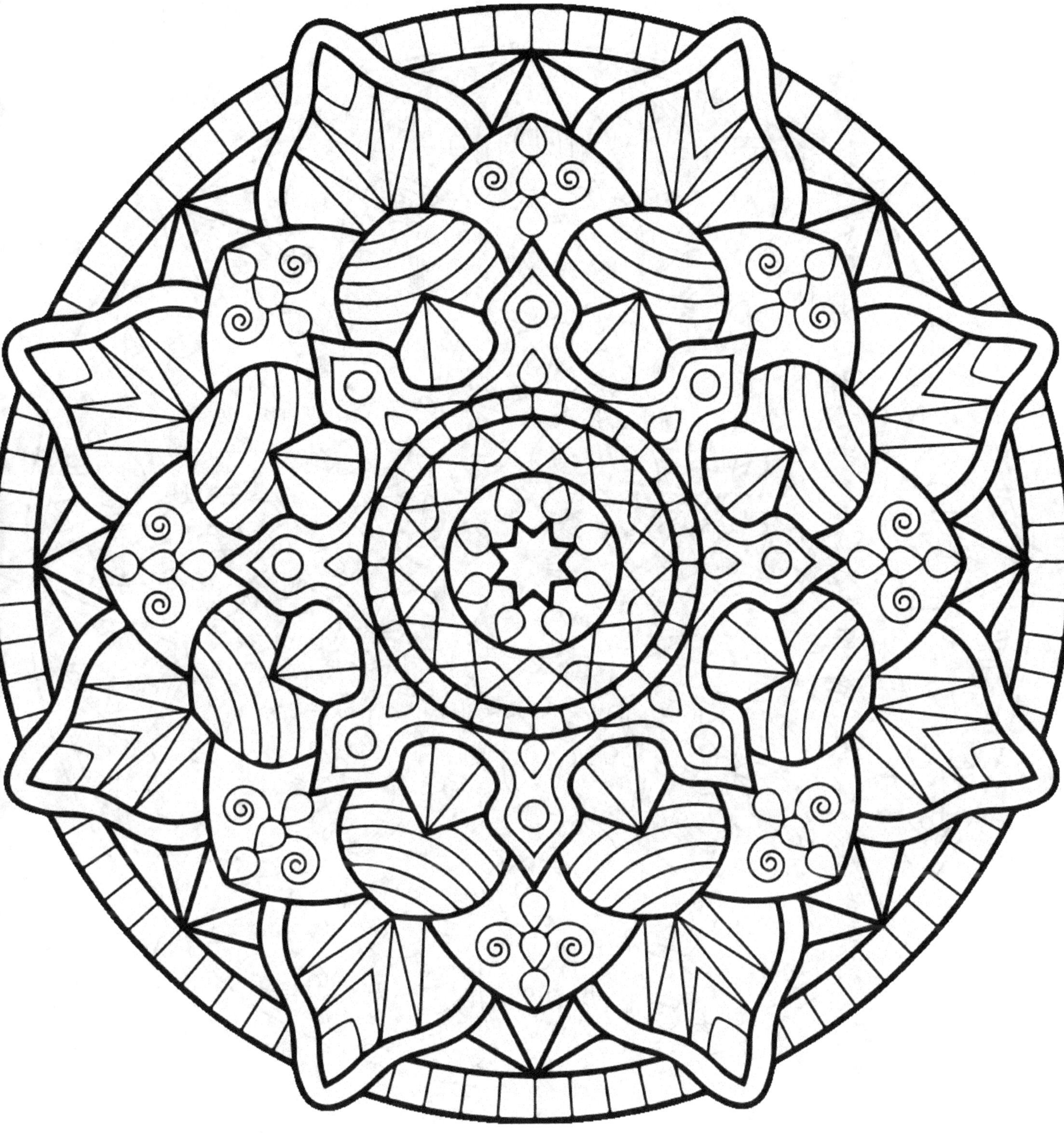

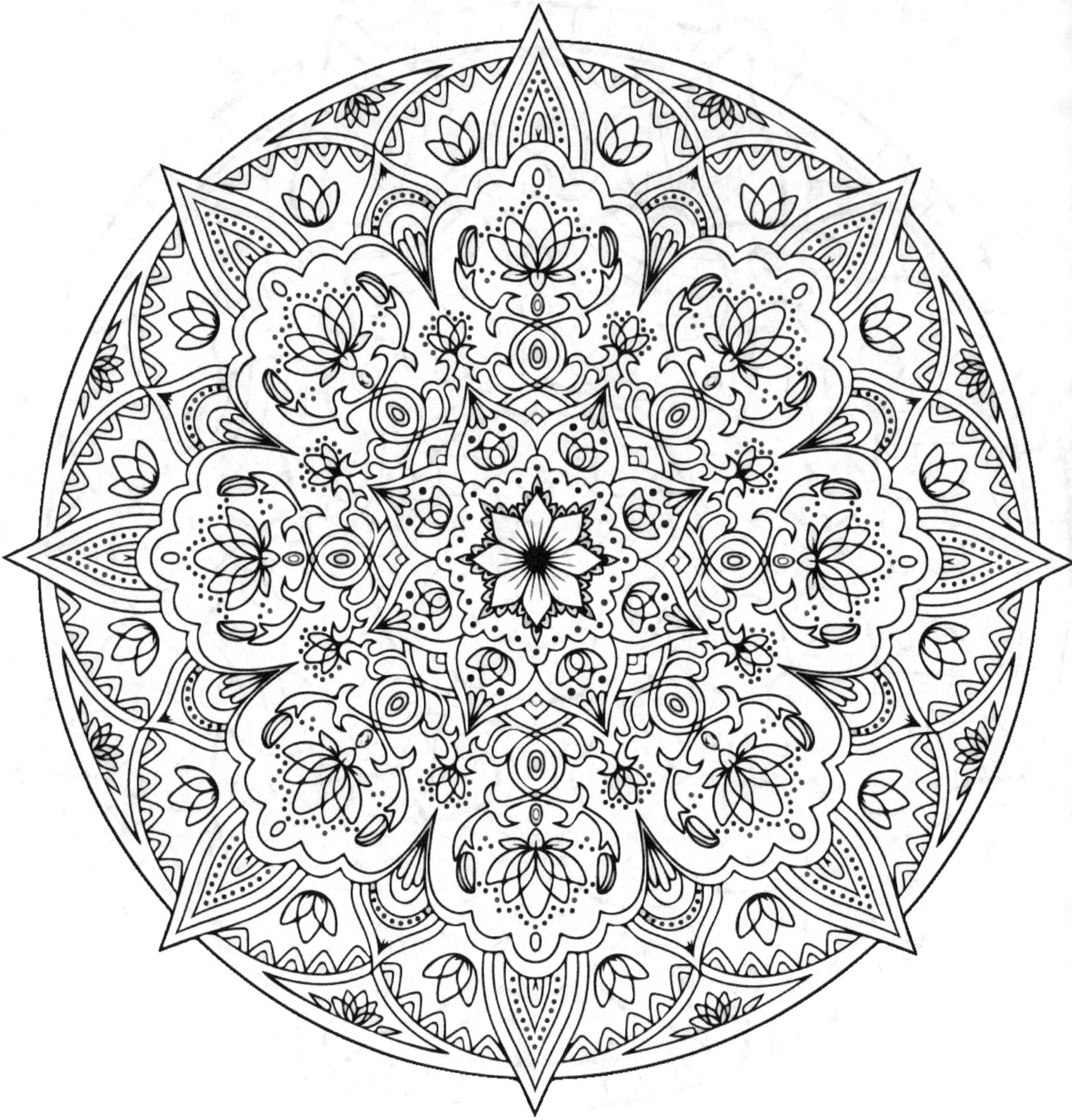

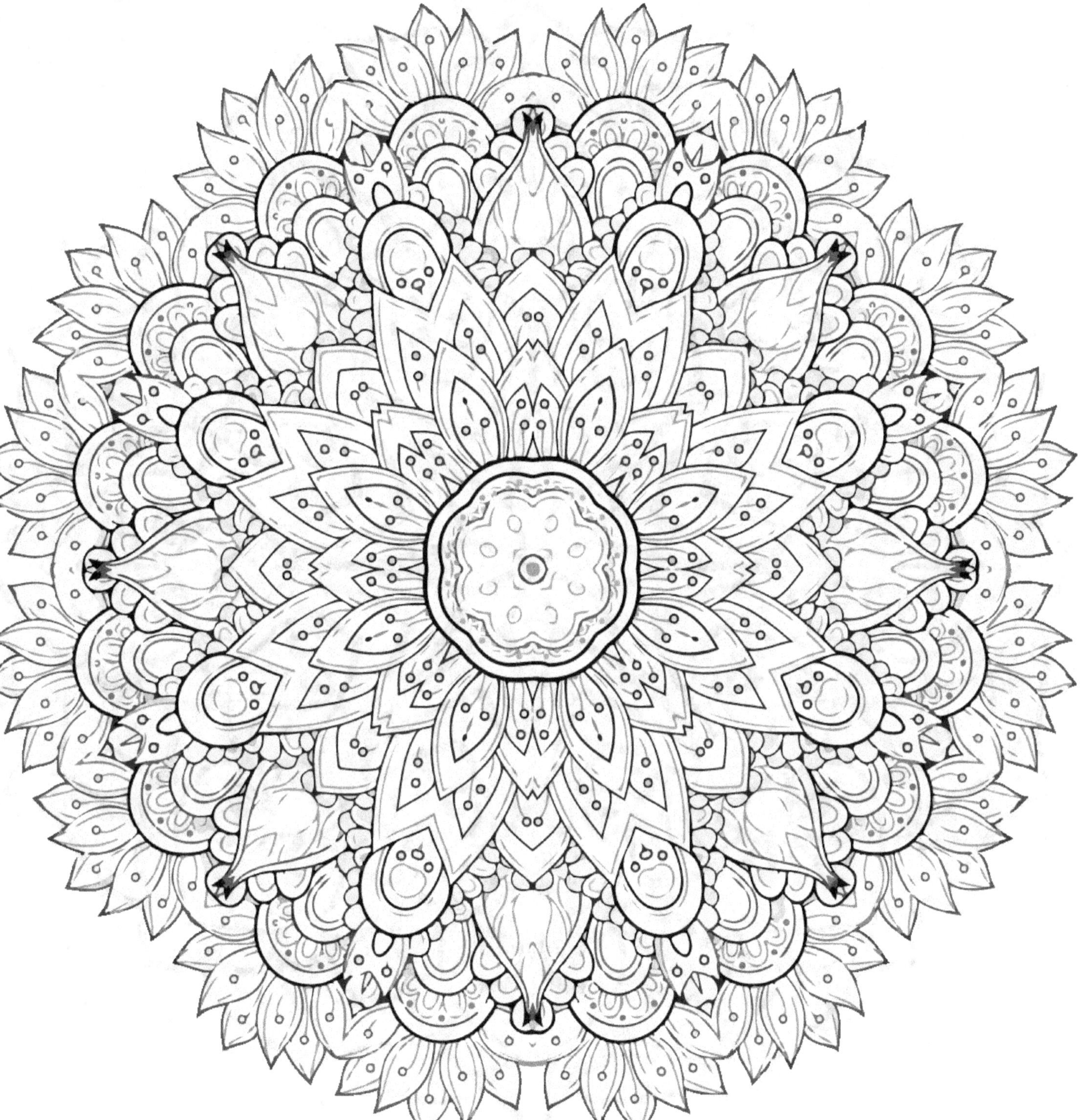

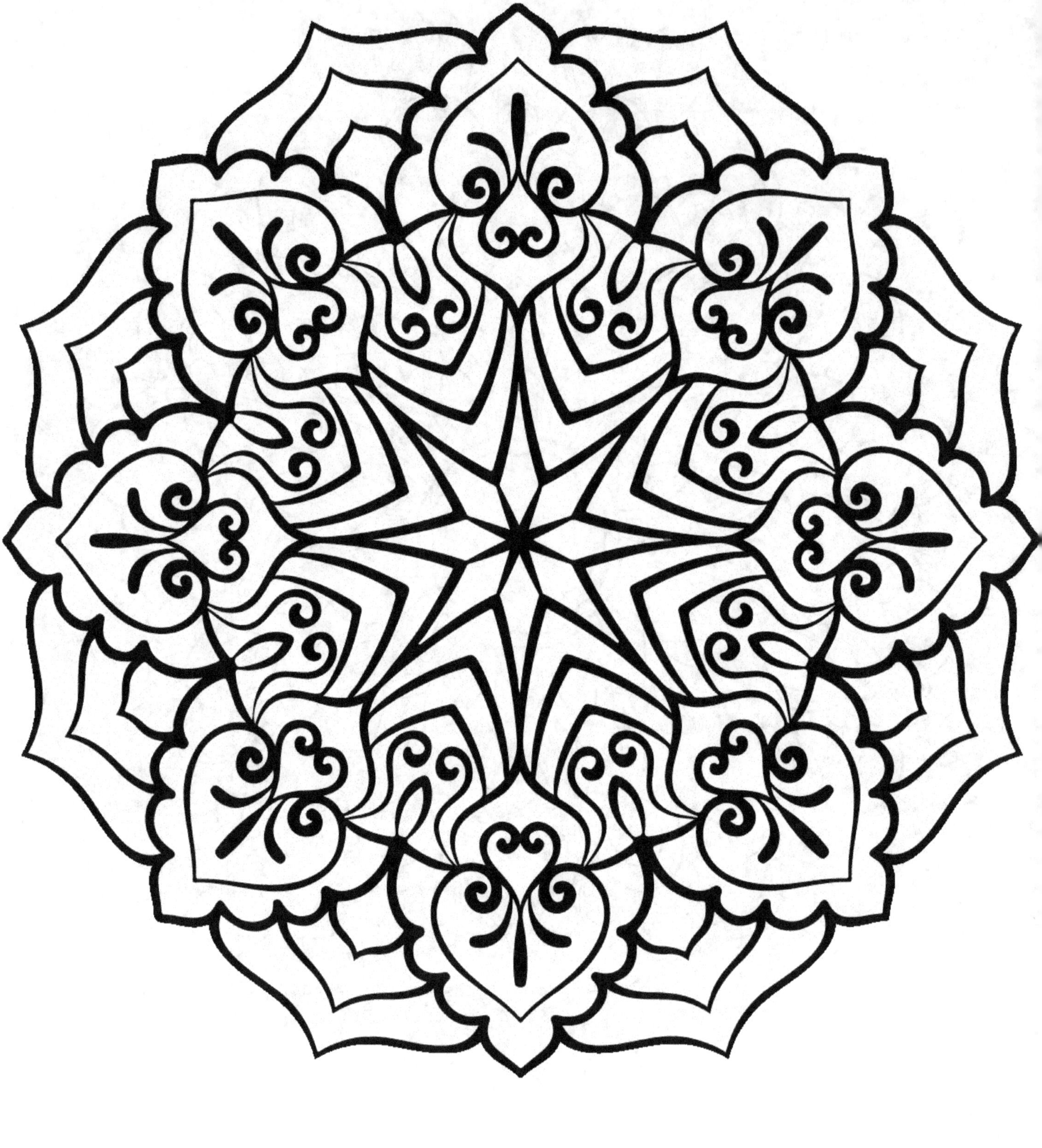

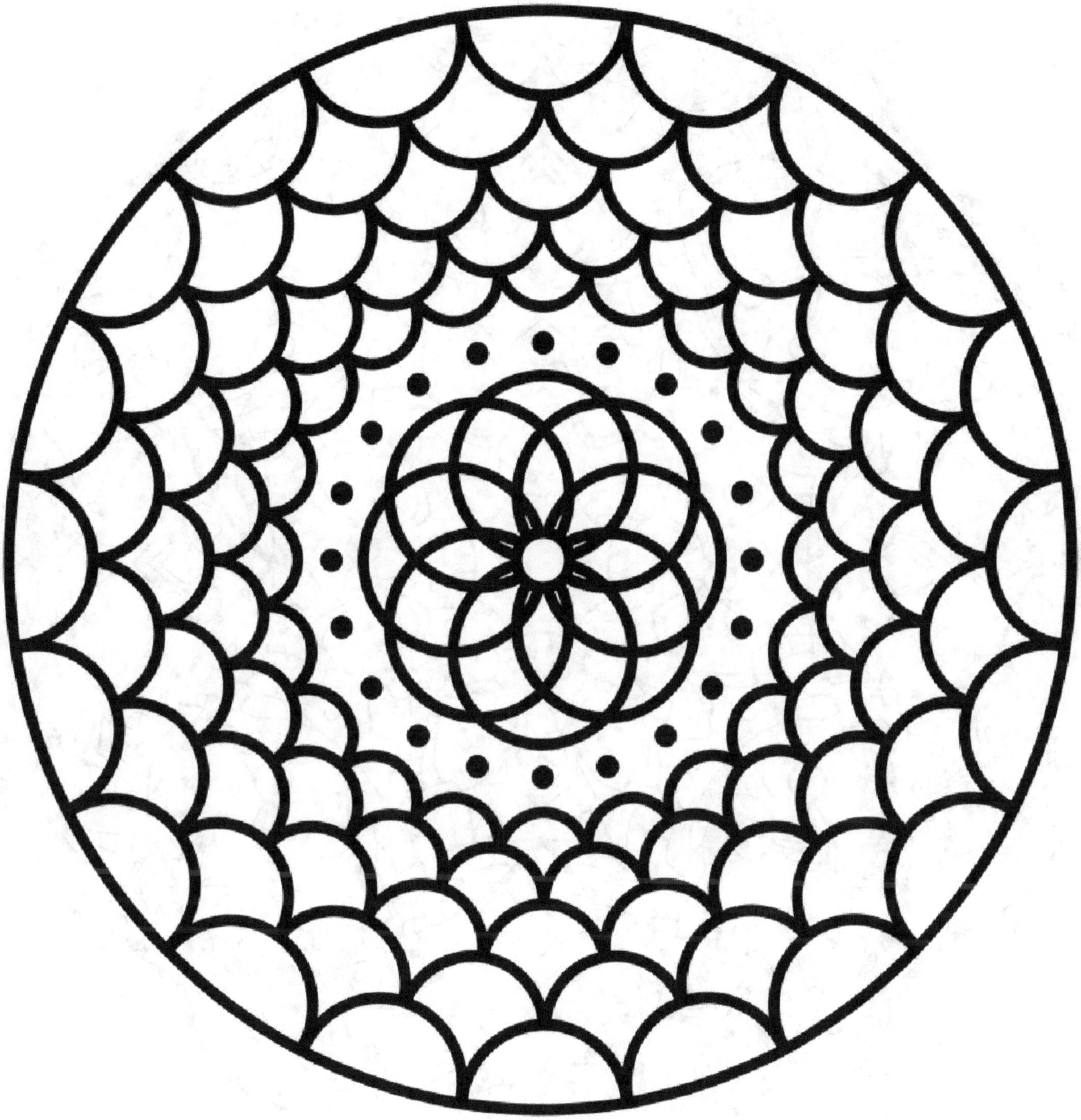

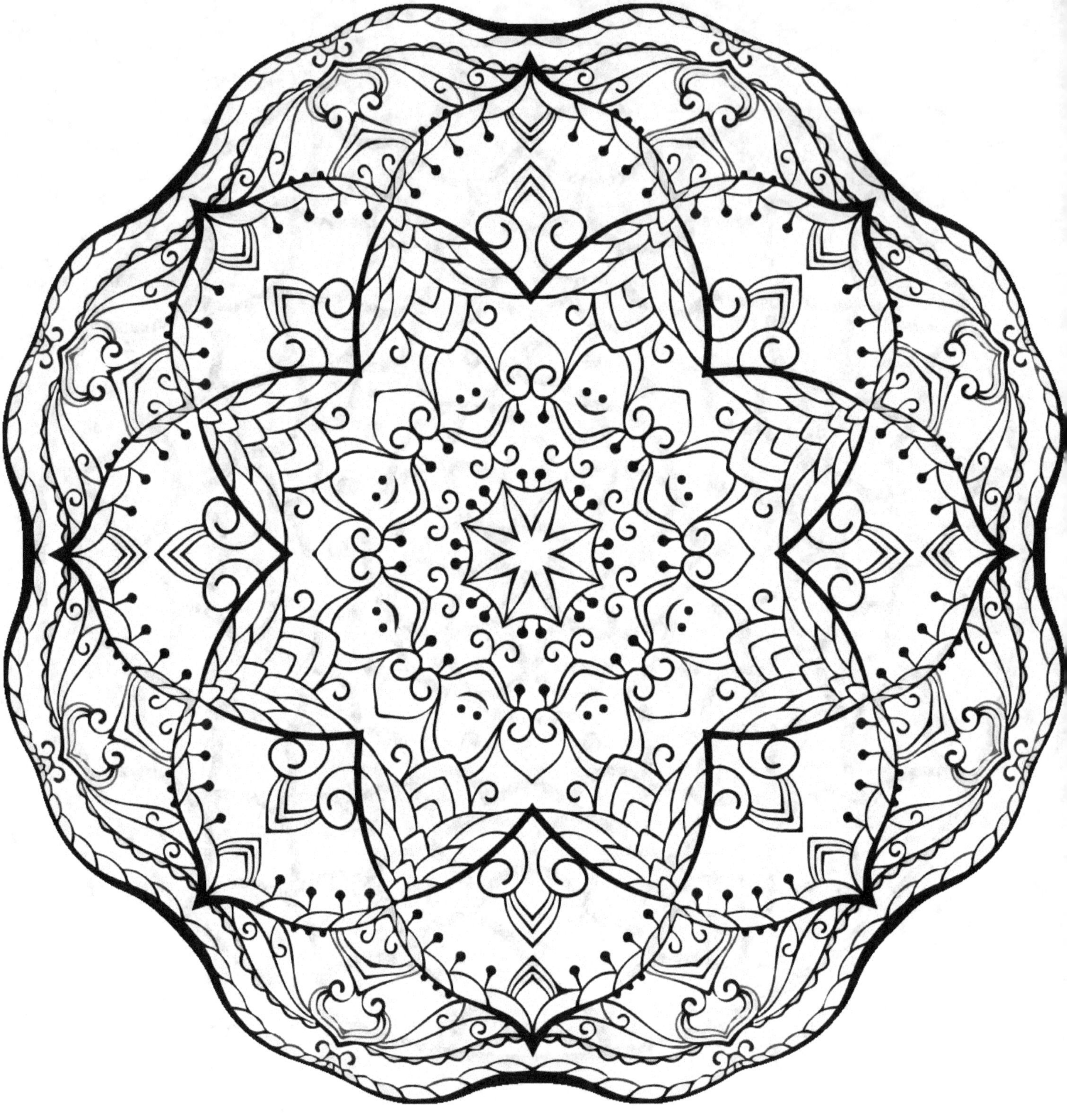

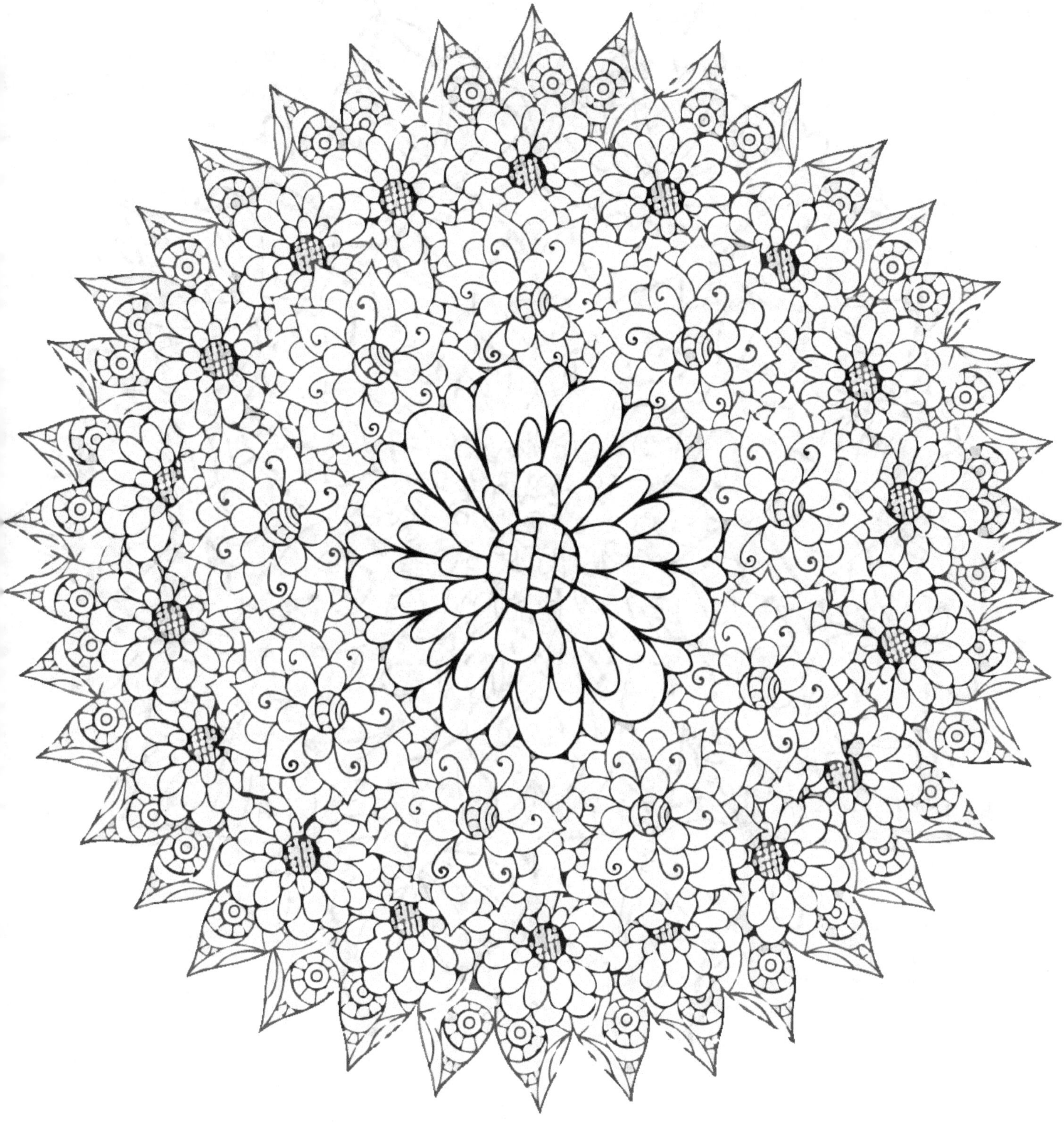

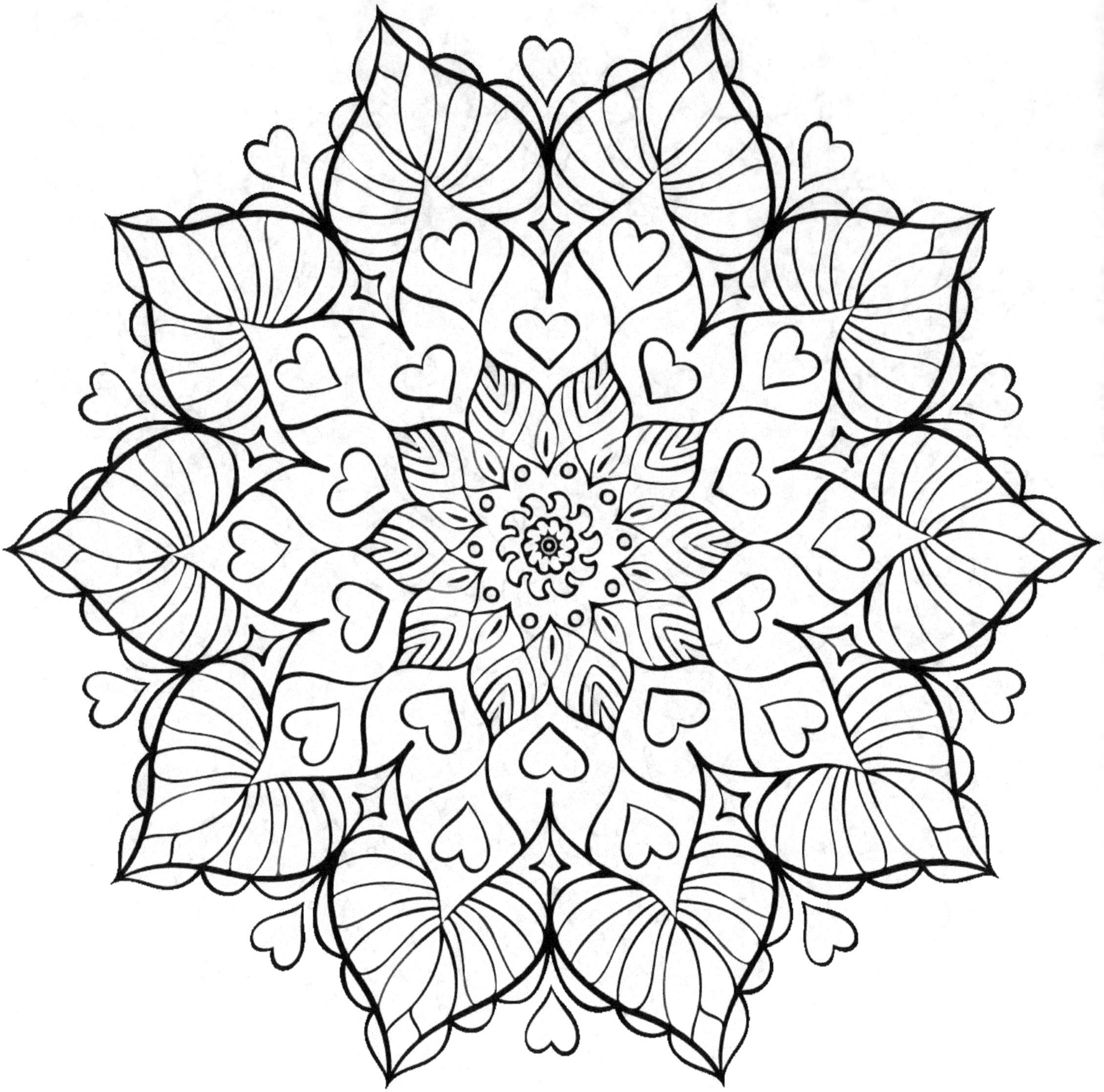

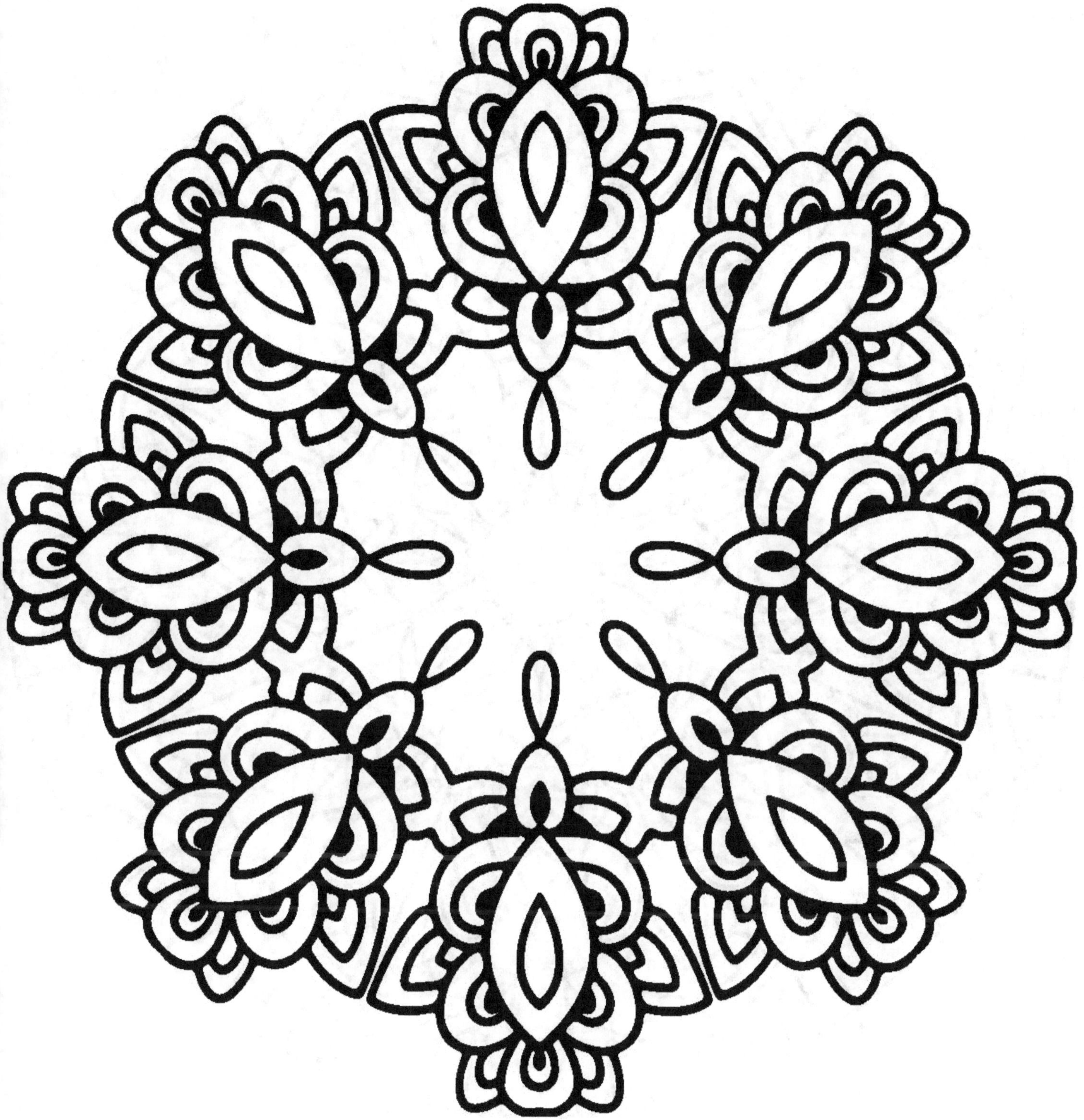

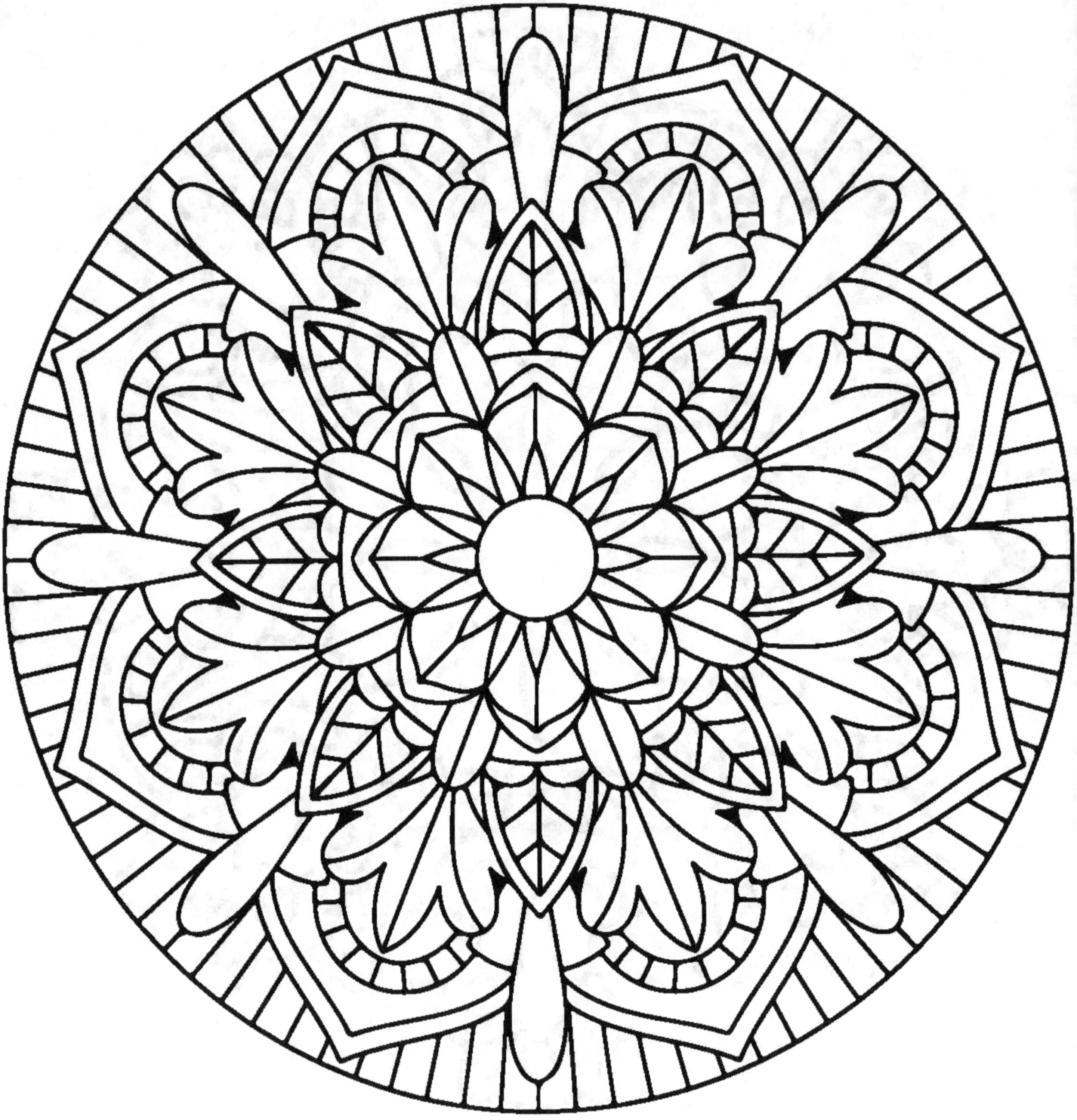

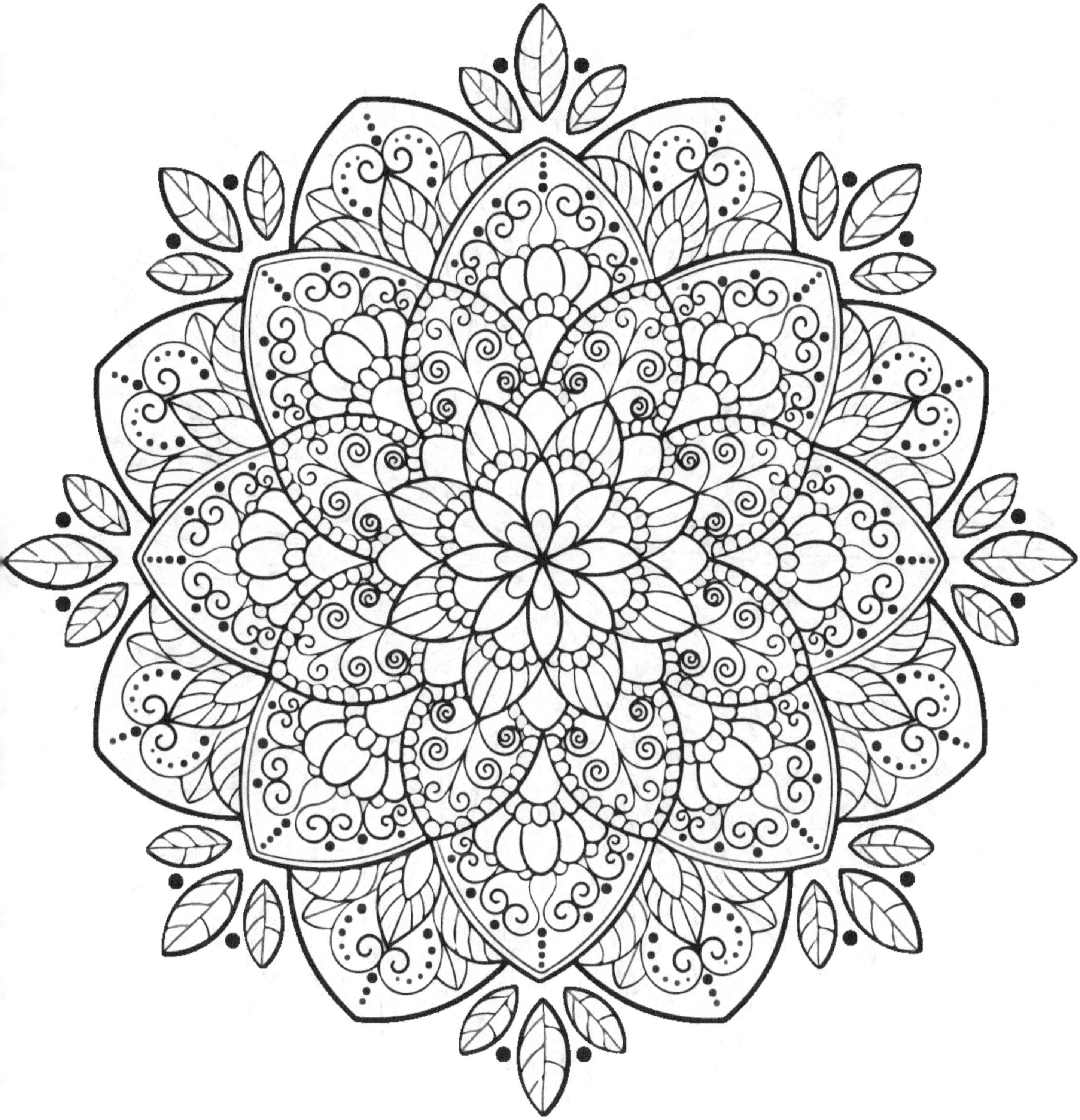

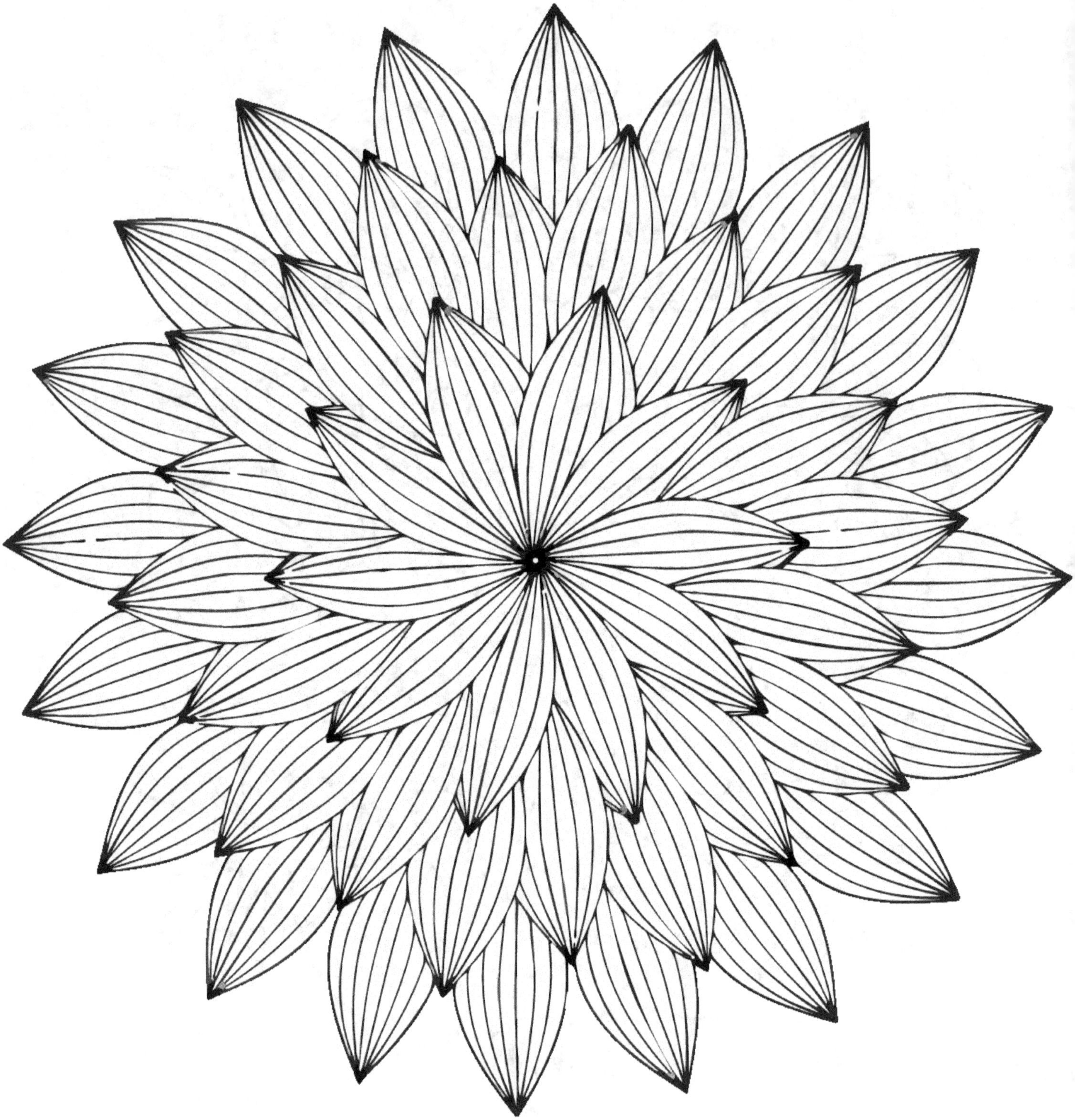

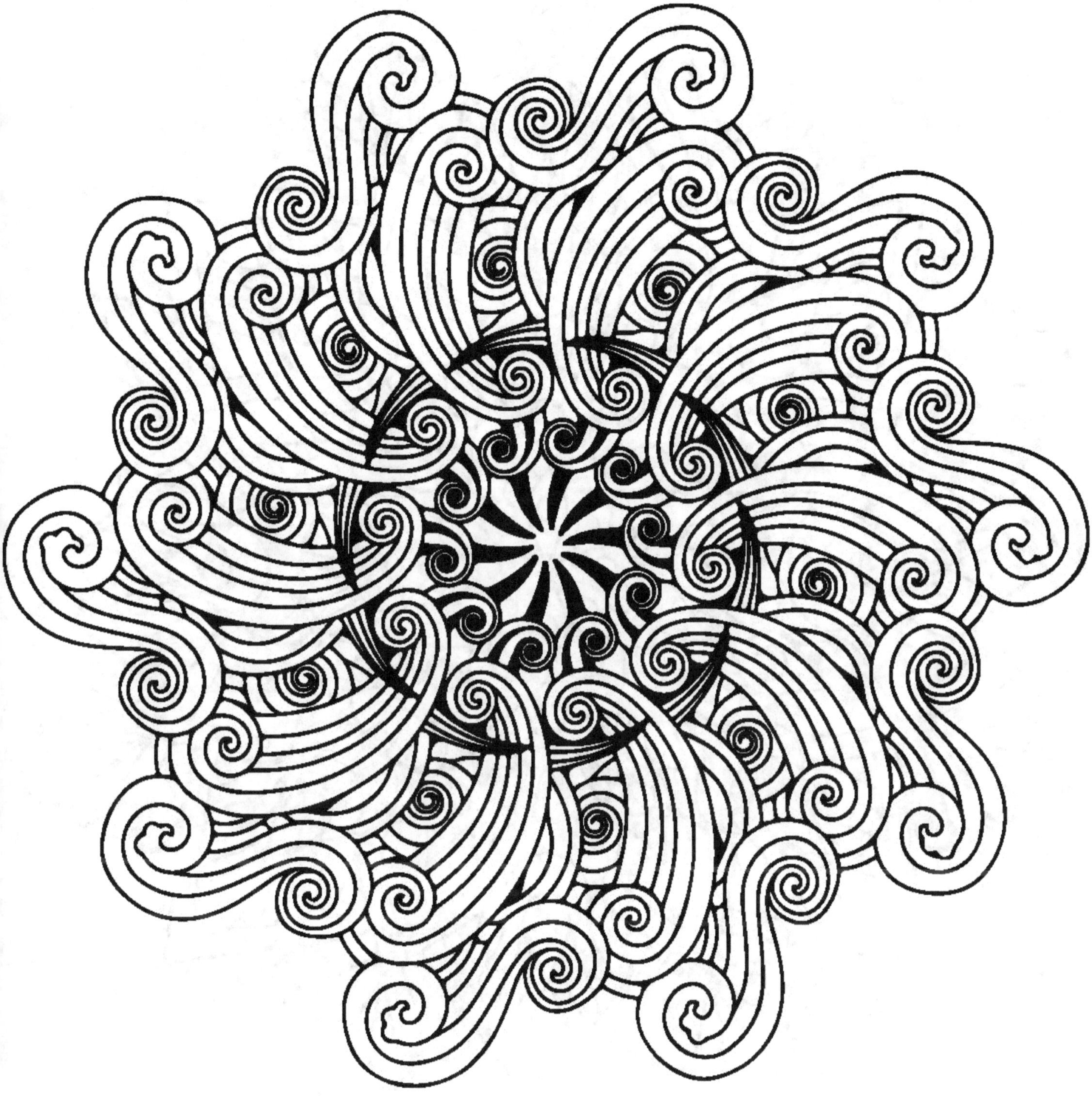

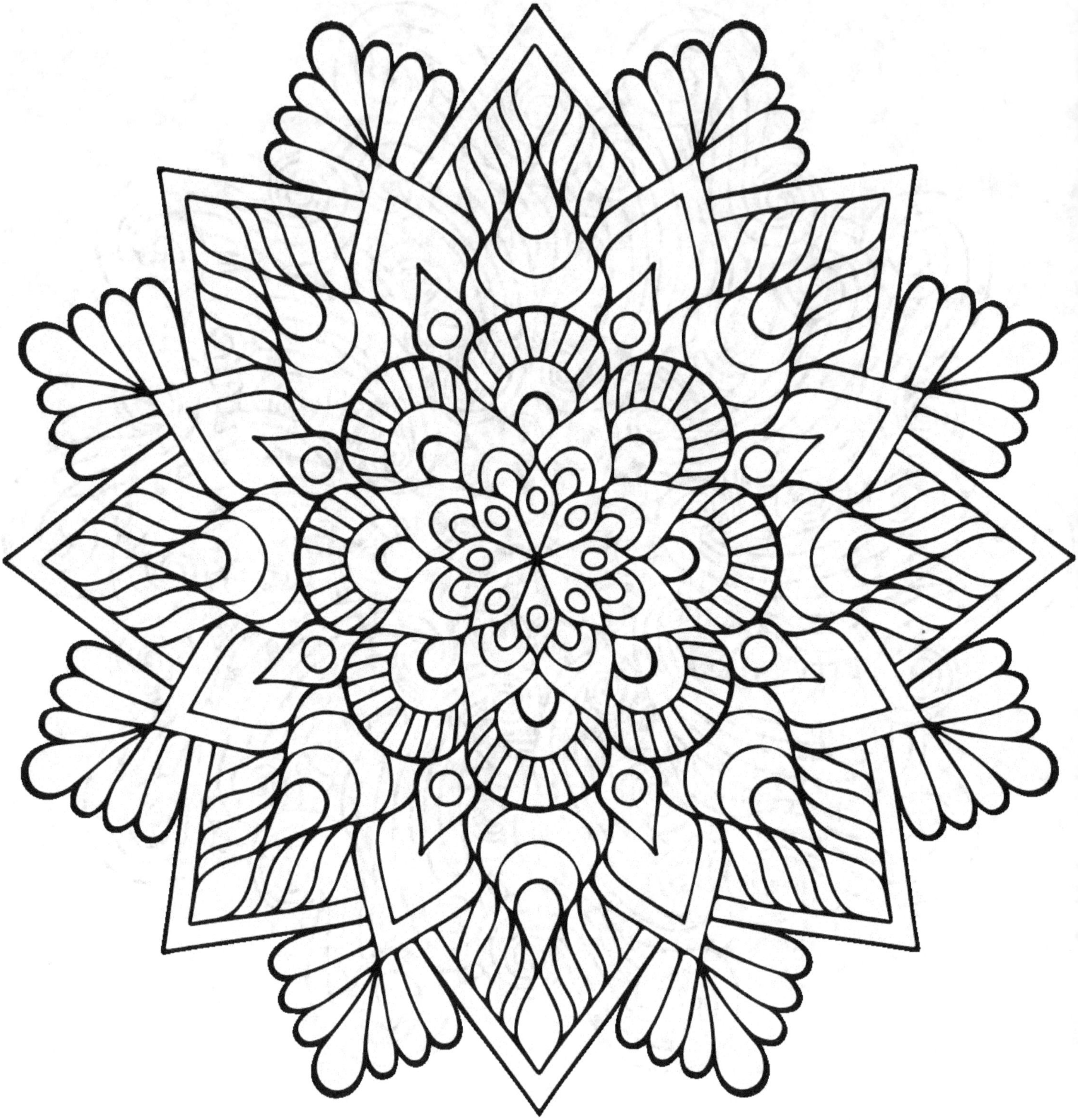

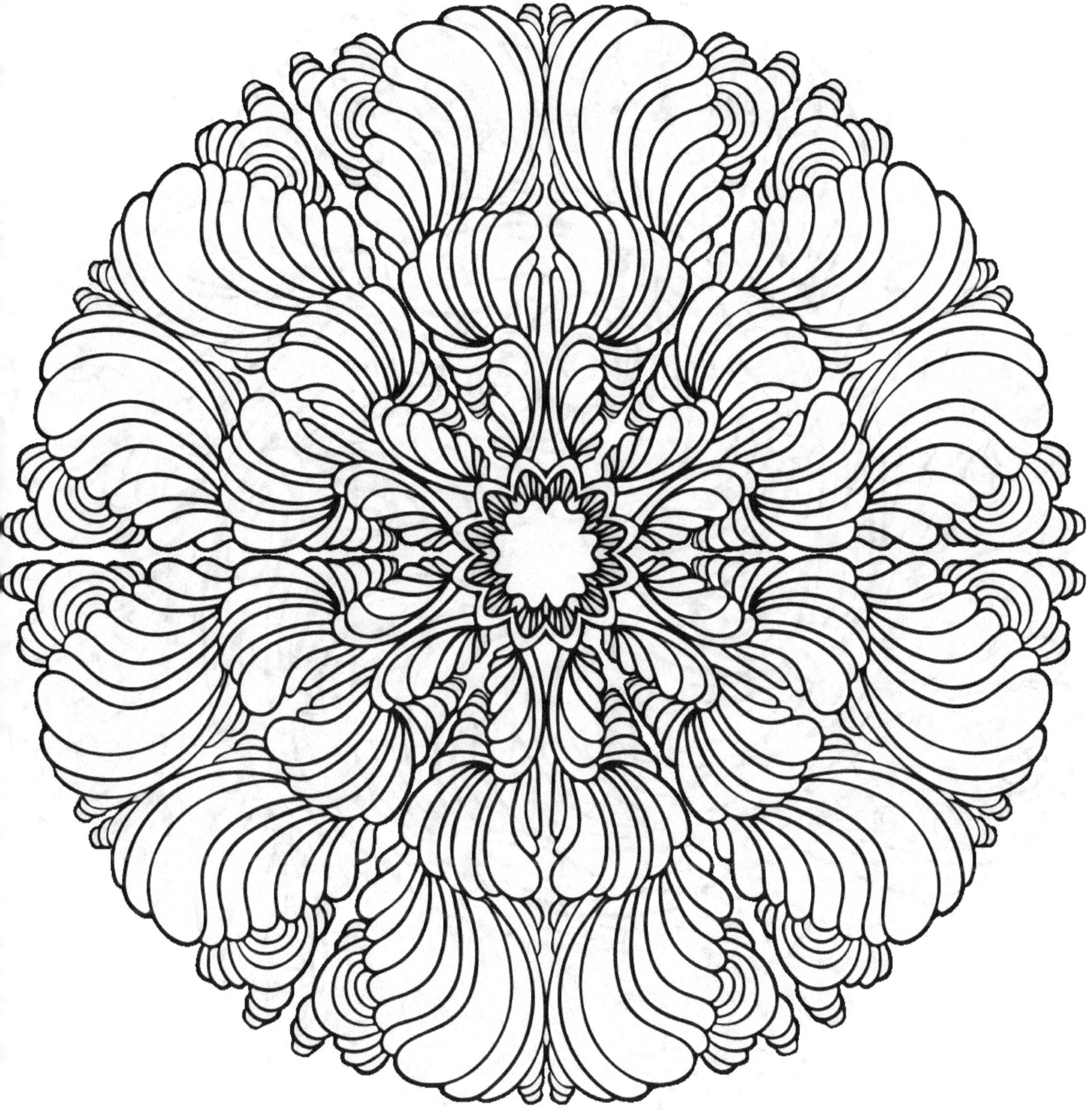

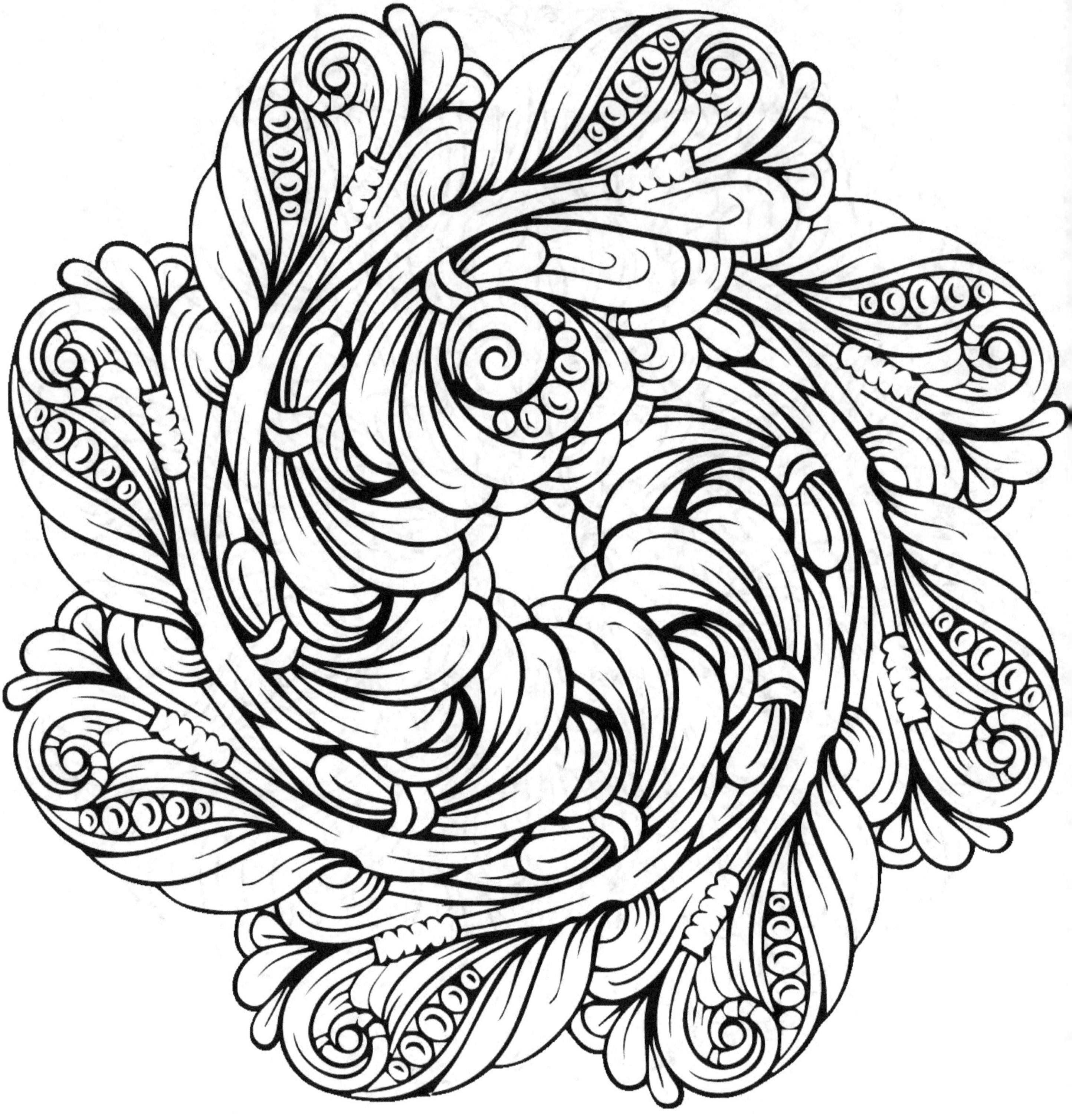

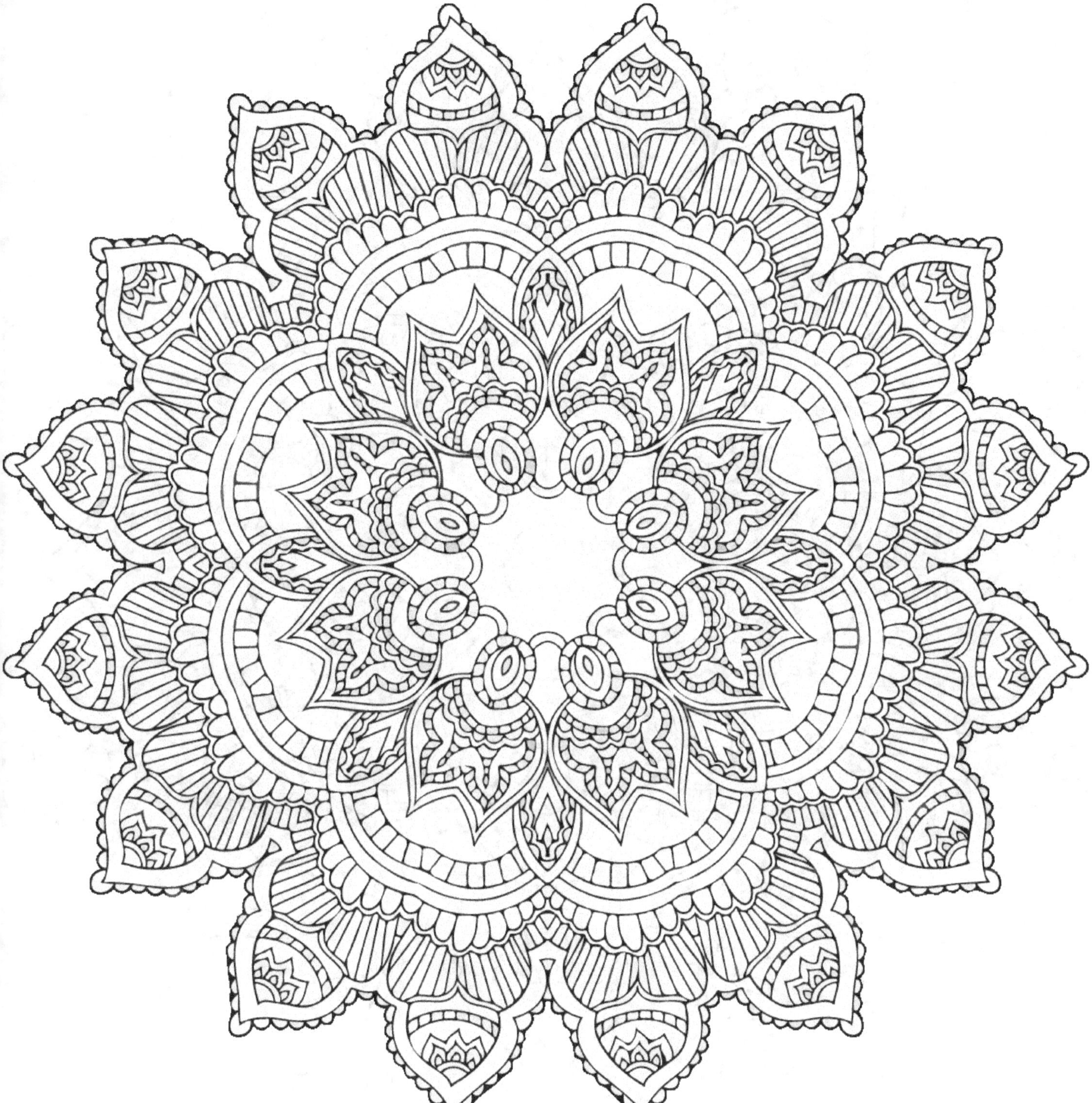

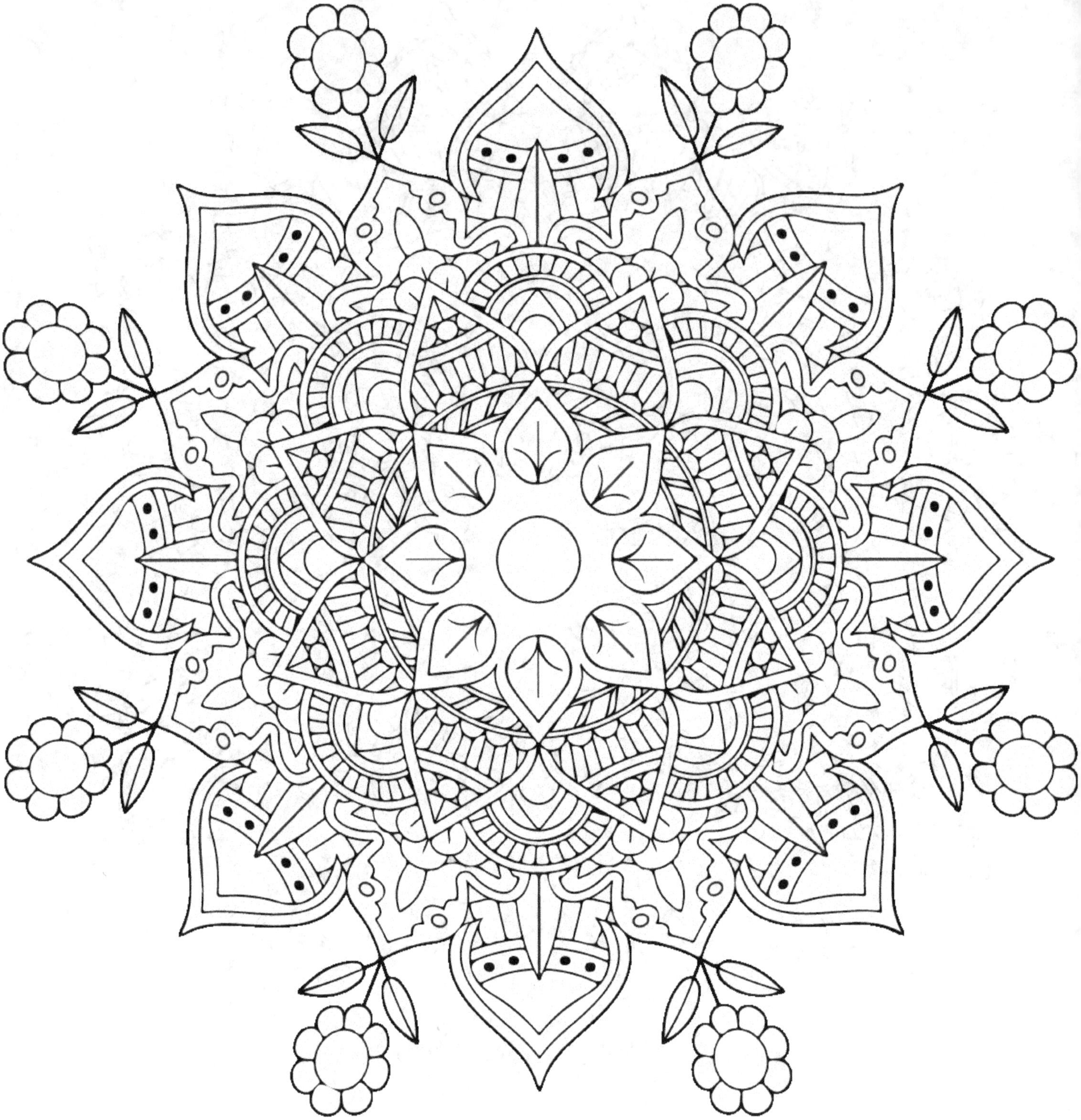

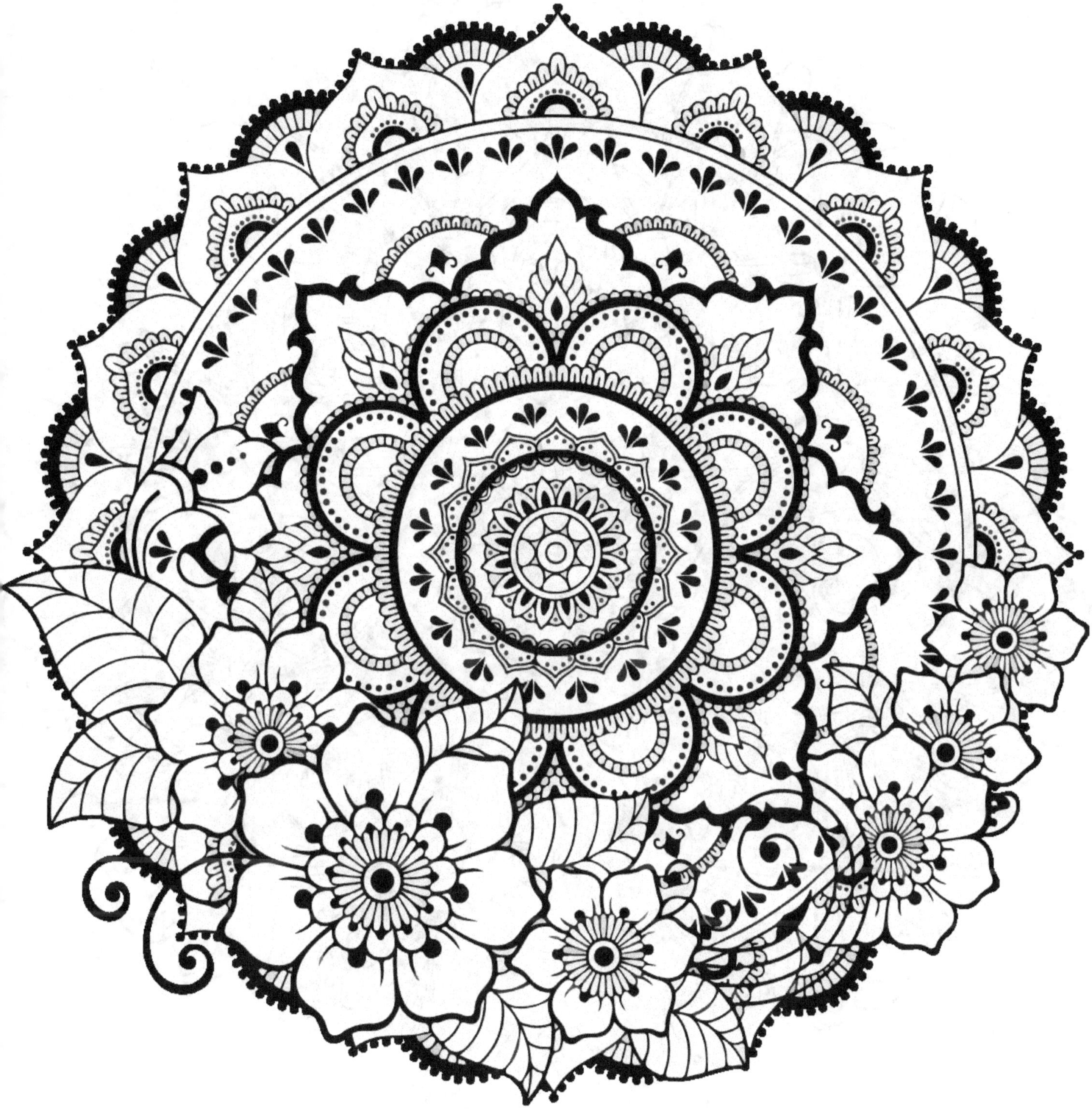

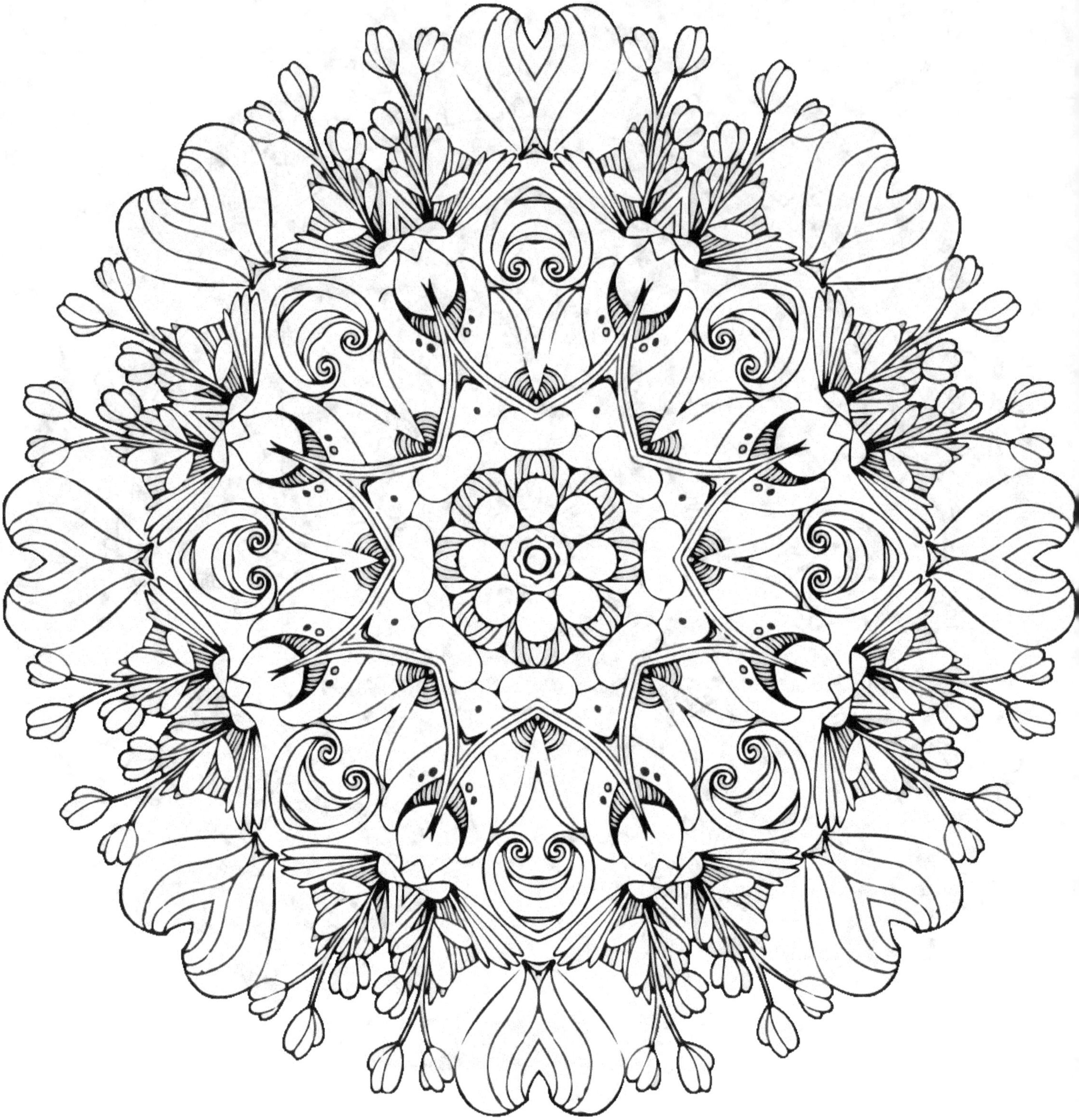

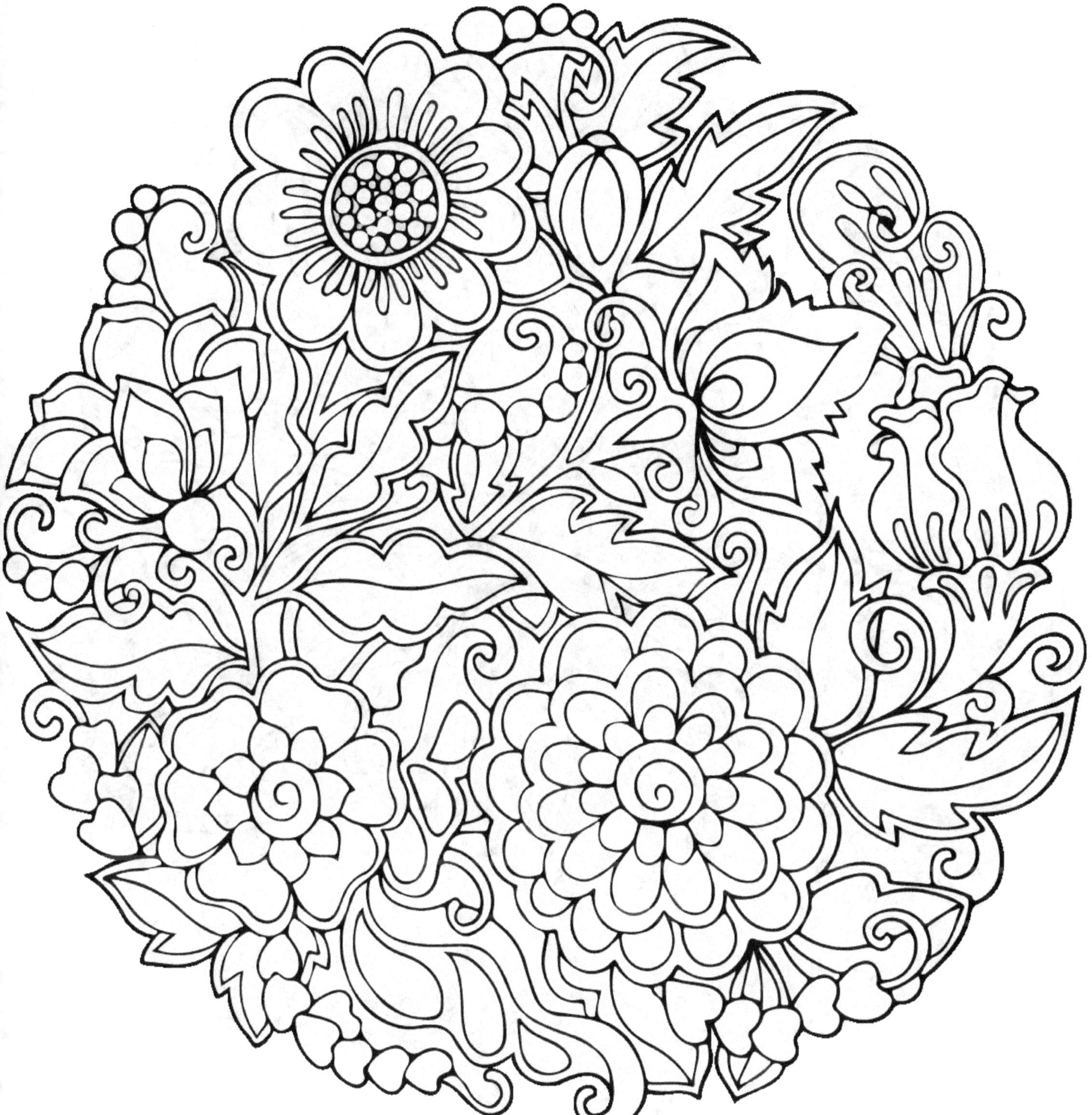

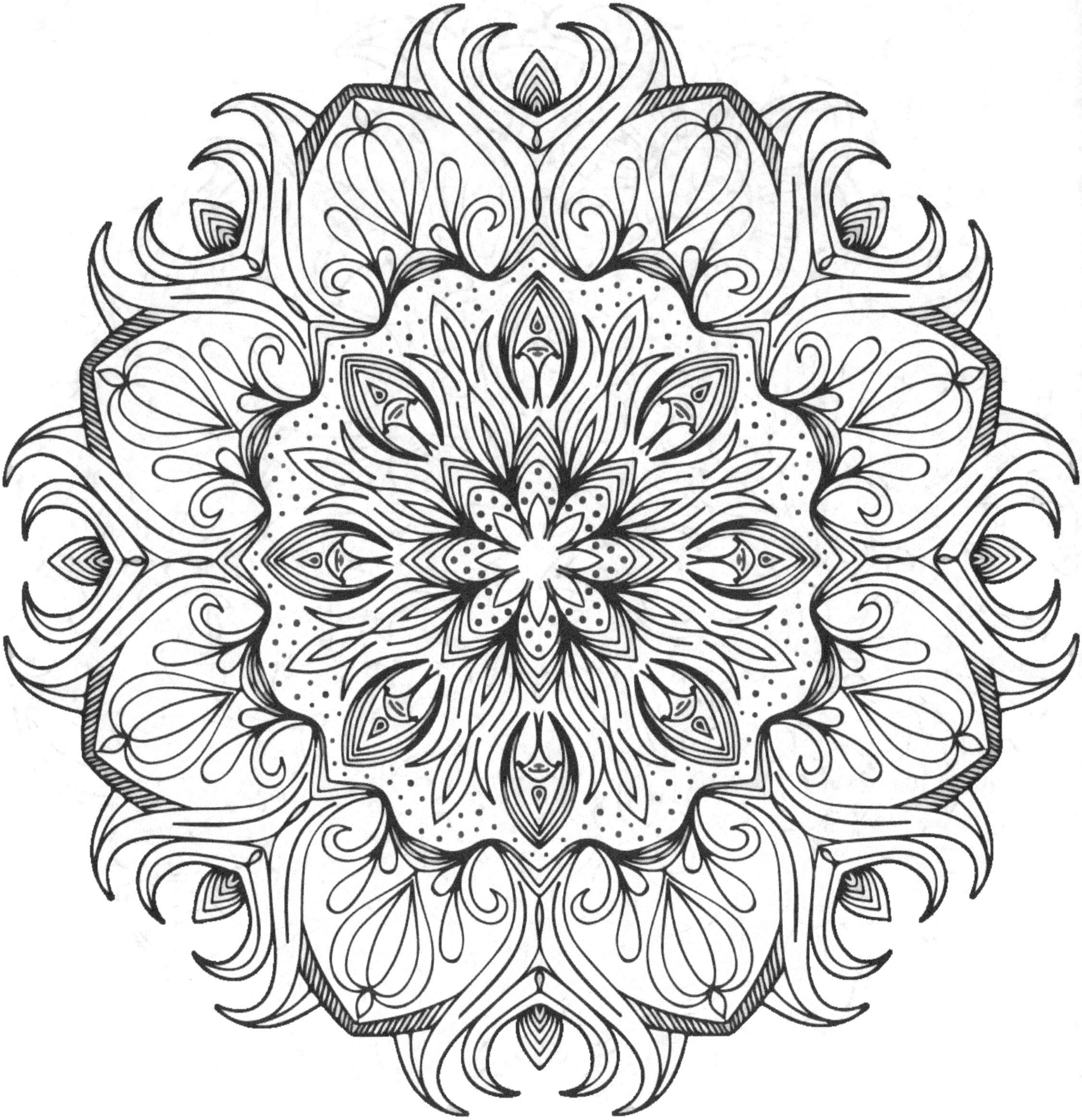

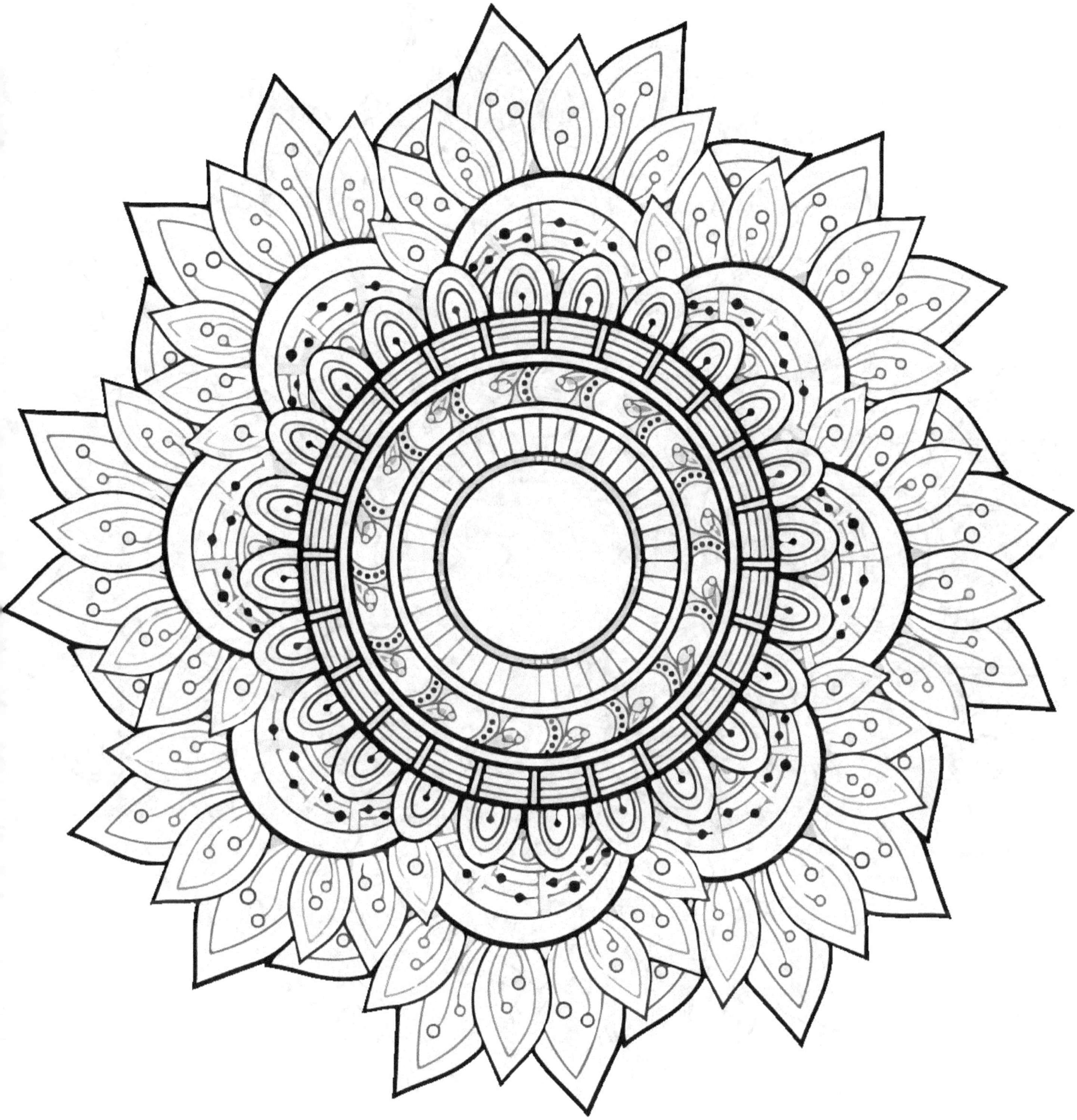

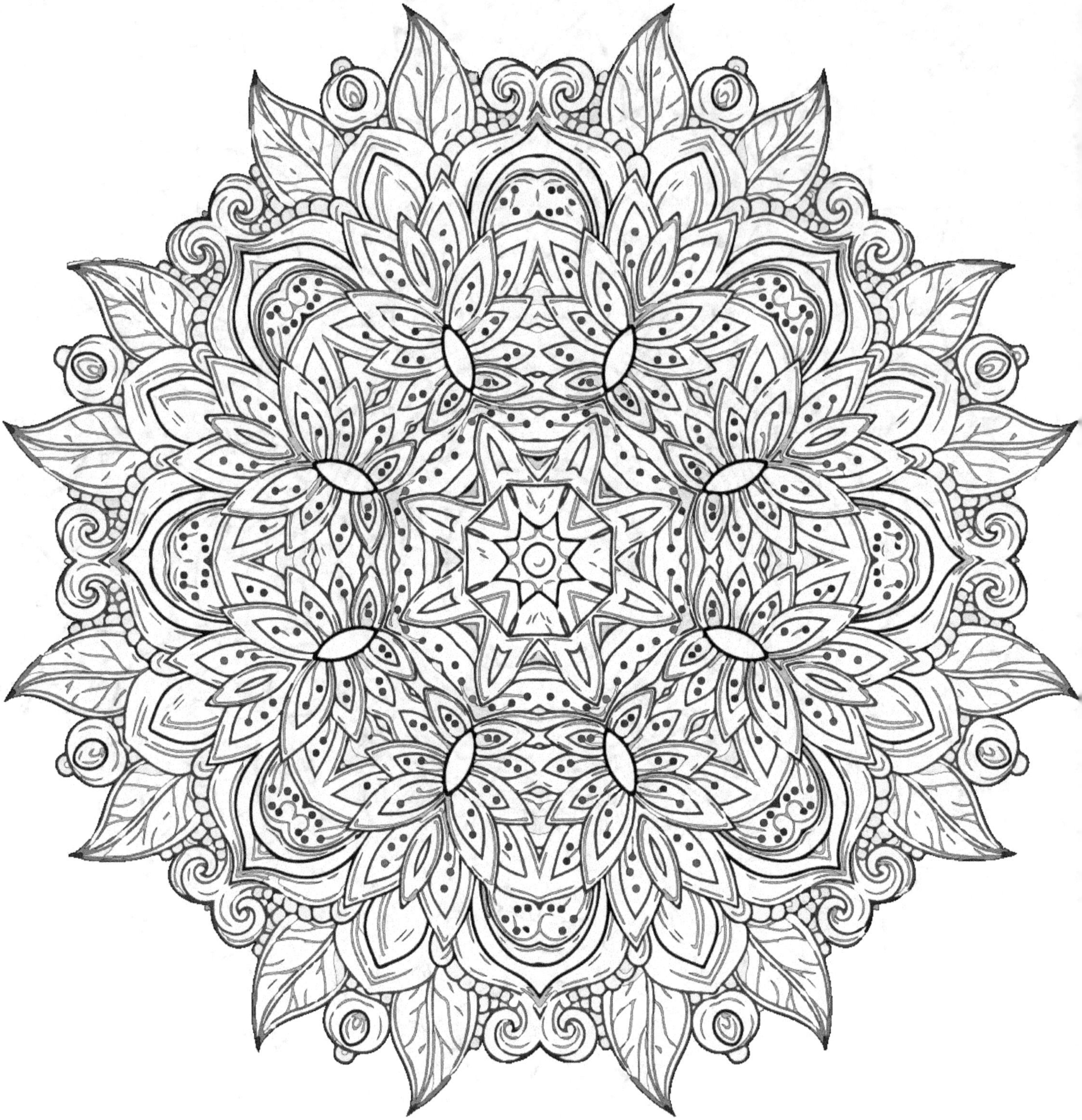

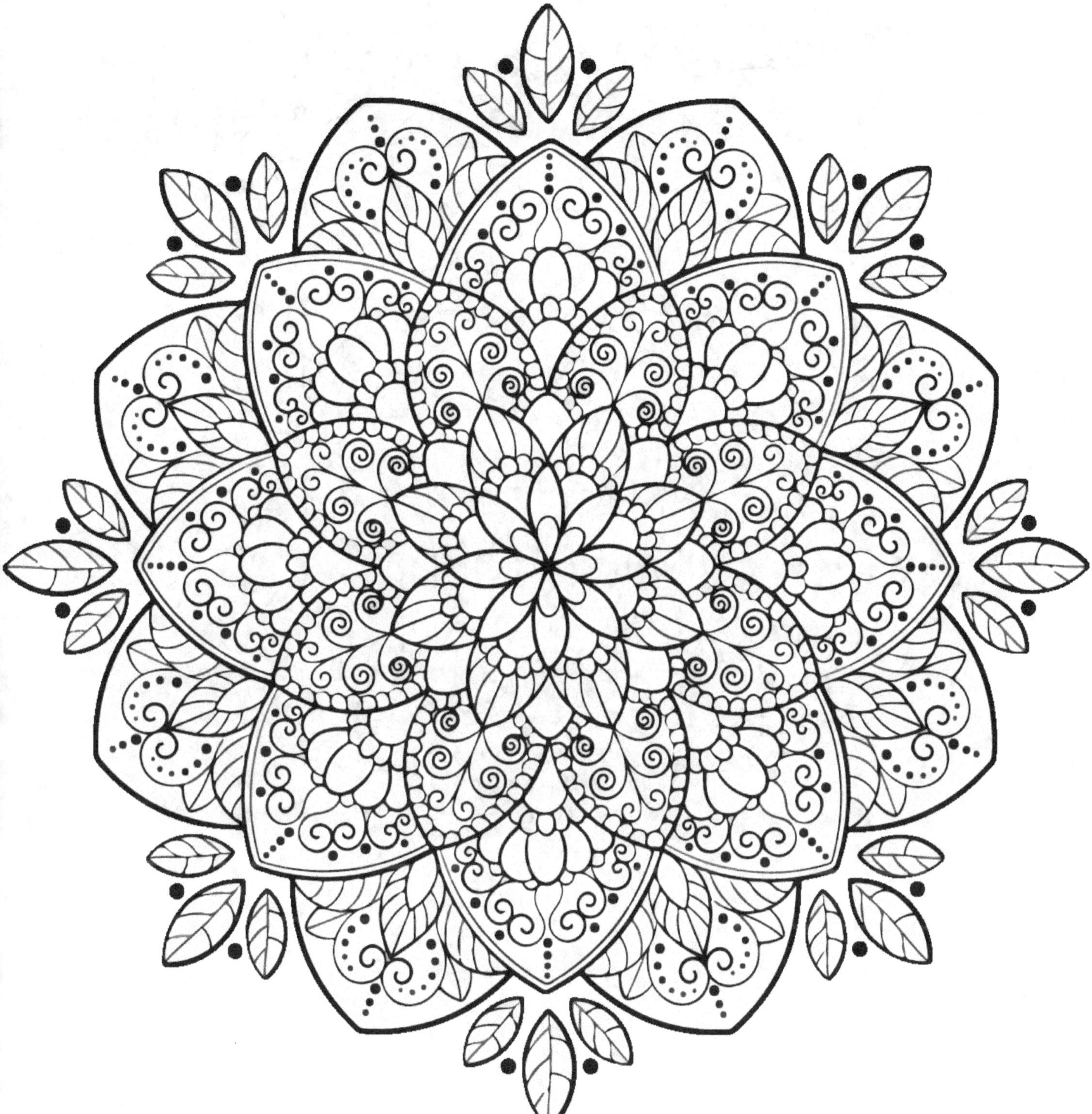

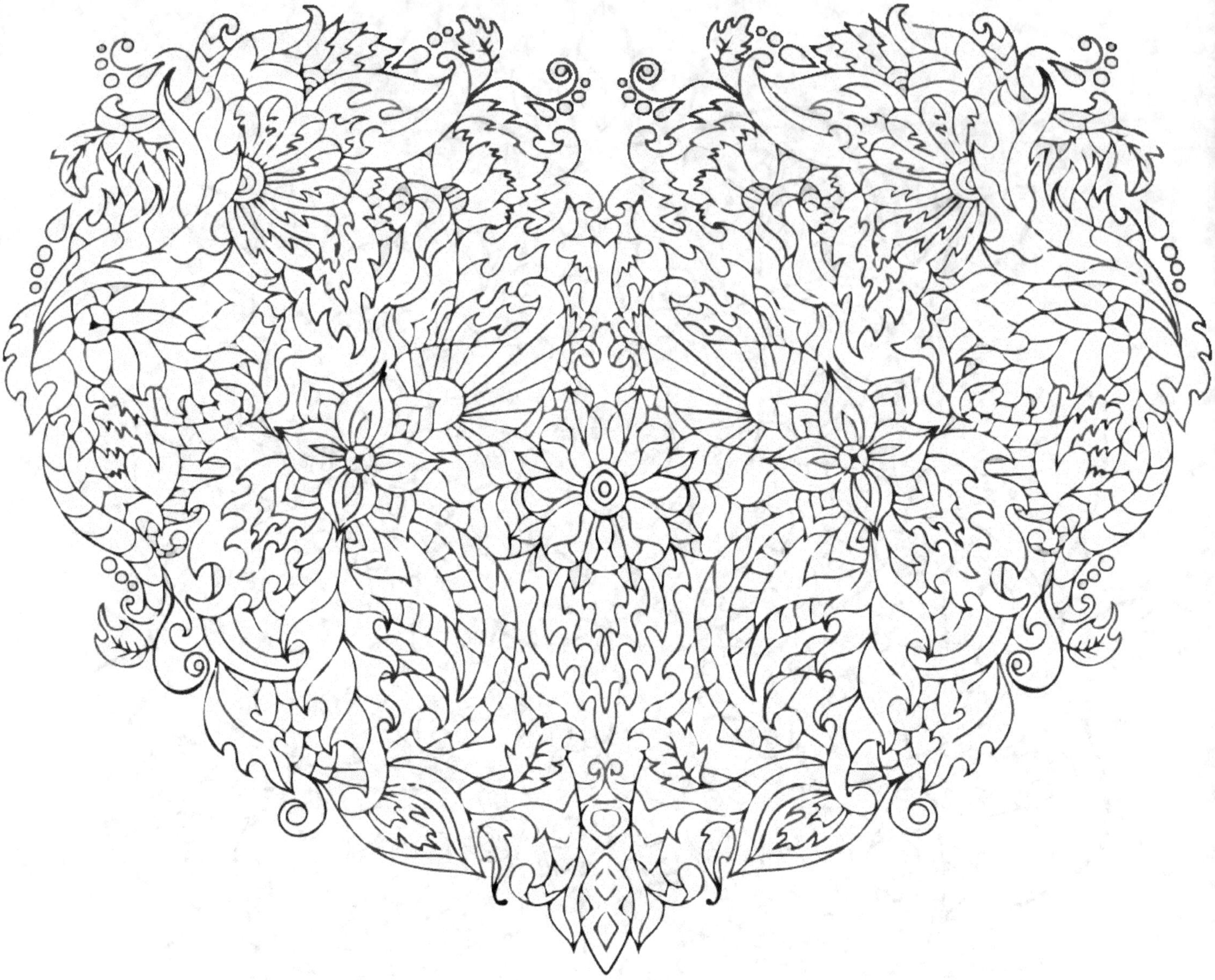

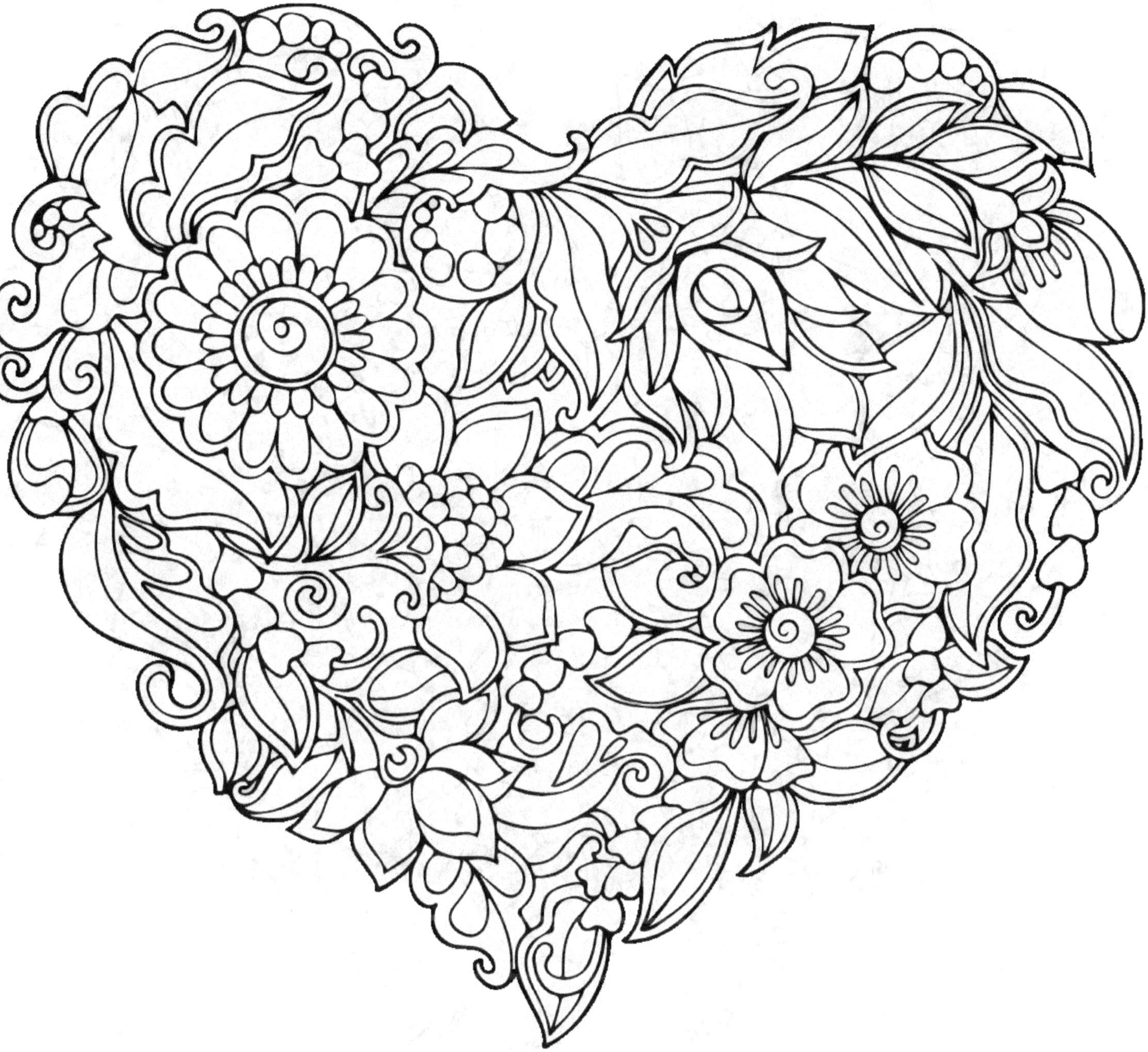

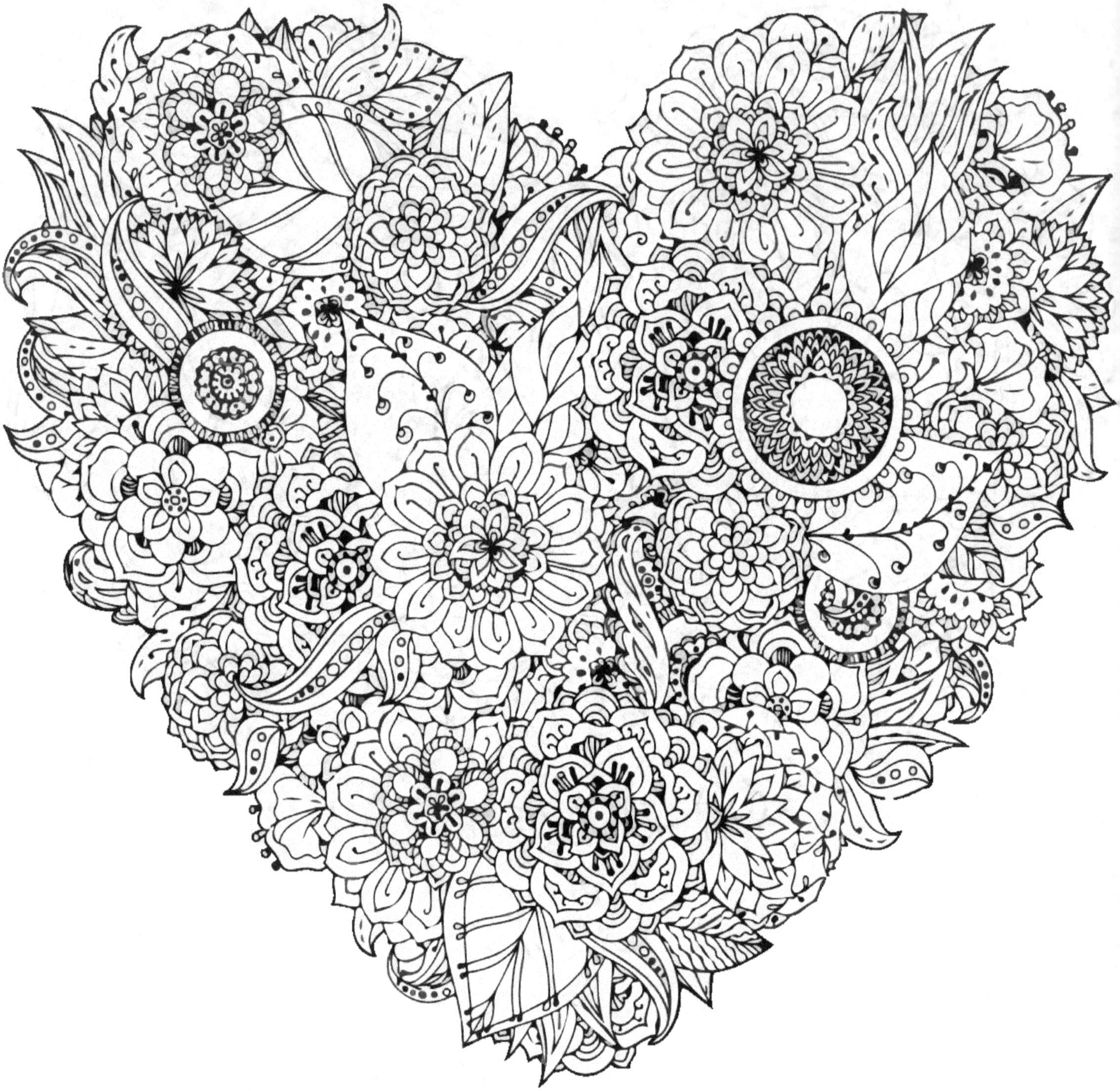

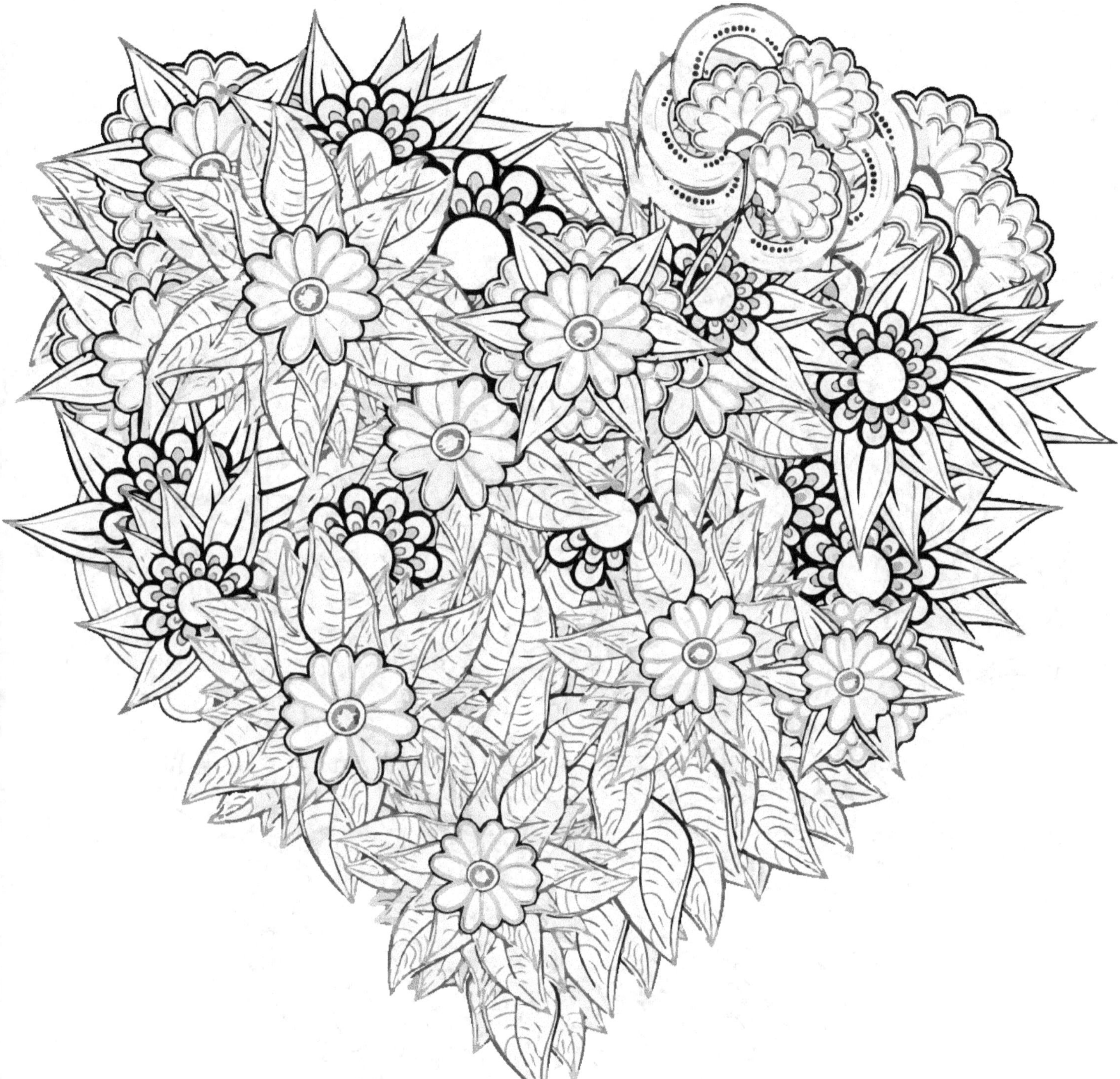

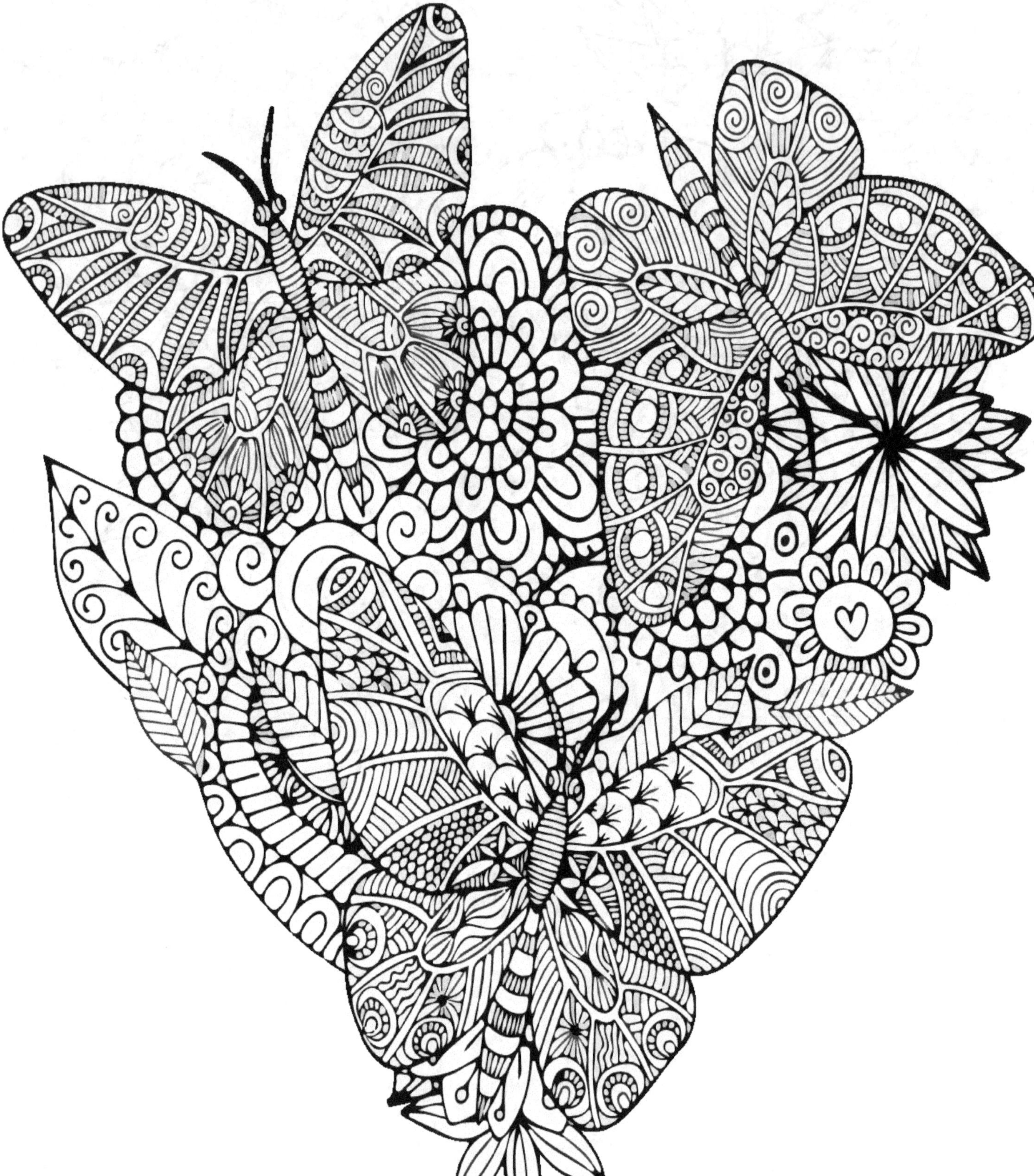

www.ingramcontent.com/pod-product-compliance
Lightning Source LLC
Chambersburg PA
CBHW060428220526
45465CB00008B/3057